Door Through Darkness

Door Through Darkness

John of the Cross
and mysticism in everyday life

Sister Eileen Lyddon

**Foreword by
Jordan Aumann, O.P.**

New City Press

For Gilbert and Alan,
with my gratitude

Published in the United States by New City Press
202 Cardinal Rd., Hyde Park, NY 12538
©1995 Sister Eileen Lyddon

First published in Great Britain by New City
57 Twyford Ave., London W3 9PZ

Library of Congress Cataloging-in-Publication Data:

Lyddon, Eileen.
    Door through darkness : John of the Cross and mysticism in
everyday life / Eileen Lyddon.

    ISBN 1-56548-037-6 (pbk.); 1-56548-044-9 (cloth)
    1. John of the Cross, Saint, 1542-1591.   2. Mysticism—Catholic
Church.   3. Catholic Church—Doctrines.   I. Title
BX4700.J7L93   1995
271'.7302—dc20   95-17643

Printed in the United States of America

Contents

Foreword

Unlike Teresa of Avila (1515-82), who was highly respected even during her lifetime as a teacher of the spiritual life and the practice of prayer, it is only in the twentieth century that her collaborator, John of the Cross (1542-91), has become widely known outside the Carmelite Order. Indeed, it was not until 1926 that he was declared a Doctor of the Church by Pope Pius XI, an event that gave an impetus to the publication of his works and prompted translators such as E. Allison Peers to make those works available to the English-speaking world.

One can think of several reasons why the spiritual teaching of John of the Cross deserves to be better known and more widely disseminated. First of all the negative aspect of Saint John's teaching has often been exaggerated by persons of a Jansenistic or fundamentalist mentality, and this has led to a distortion of his doctrine. Secondly, in the secular, individualistic and sensate culture of contemporary society, it is very difficult to promote spiritual values or to get people to practice the asceticism and detachment that are necessary for living an authentic Christian life. John of the Cross is able to meet that challenge.

To have a correct understanding of the spiritual doctrine of John of the Cross, one must be aware that he is the author not only of *The Ascent of Mount Carmel* and *The Dark Night of the*

Soul, but also of *The Spiritual Canticle* and *The Living Flame of Love.* In other words, his spiritual teaching encompasses the entire scope of the spiritual life, from its ascetical beginnings to the loftiest degrees of the mystical union. Whereas spiritual authors such as Ignatius of Loyola and Francis de Sales concentrated on the ascetical aspect of conversion, Christian commitment, and growth in virtue, John of the Cross is much more comprehensive. His intention from the very beginning is to encourage and assist souls to reach the summit. He says as much in the prologue to *The Ascent of Mount Carmel:*

> Wherefore, to the end that all, whether beginners or proficients, may know how to commit themselves to God's guidance when His Majesty desires to lead them onward, we shall give instruction and counsel, by his help, so that they may be able to understand his will or, at the least, allow him to lead them. . . . Of all these, with the divine favor, we shall endeavor to say something, so that each soul who reads this may be able to see something of the road that he ought to follow, if he aspires to attain to the summit of this Mount (4, 7, Peers translation).

John of the Cross did not propose detachment and self-denial as ends in themselves, although numerous persons have interpreted his teaching in that negative sense. Ascetical practices are simply the means, although a necessary means, for conversion to God and total submission to his will. Jesus himself is the source of the Christian teaching on self-denial and detachment: "If a man wishes to come after me, he must deny his very self, take up his cross, and follow in my steps" (Mk 8:34). This teaching is nicely balanced by another statement of Christ: "I came that they might have life and have it to the full" (Jn 10:11).

Not only is the teaching of John of the Cross an authentic

gospel teaching; it is one that is sorely needed in our time, as is evident from the ever-increasing number of persons who are seeking guidance and inspiration from the Carmelite school of spirituality. For example, the teaching of John of the Cross on active purgation in *The Ascent of Mount Carmel* can be an effective therapy for curing the addictive behavior of all too many persons in our sensate culture.

That alone is sufficient reason to be sincerely grateful to Sister Eileen Lyddon for her masterly exposition and commentary on the spiritual doctrine of John of the Cross. Six of the eight chapters of her book deal with the active purgation of the senses and spirit, and rightly so, since it is at the first stages, in the passage through the night, that one especially needs guidance and instruction. And for those who would otherwise find the terminology of John of the Cross unfamiliar and his literary style somewhat academic, Sister Eileen's book can serve as an excellent introduction to the writings of the Mystical Doctor. As she says: "This book has been written for beginners who want to read the words of John of the Cross himself rather than accounts of his teaching by others" (Introduction, p. 18).

Jordan Aumann, O.P.
Dominican Priory, River Forest, Illinois

Mount Carmel

There is no way here for to the righteous there is no law, since he is a law to himself

delight   wisdom   justice

nothing gives me glory   happiness   joy   peace

Jer II I brought you into the land of Carmel, to eat the fruit thereof, and the goodness thereof.

The honour and glory of God alone dwell on this mount

strength   love   godliness   nothing gives me pain

The more I wished to have the less I possessed

nor that — nor that — nor that — nor that — nor that — nor that

How that I wish for nothing I have all without wishing

Way of imperfection with regard to heavenly things: glory, joy, knowledge, consolation, rest

The path of Mount Carmel: spirit of perfection, nothing nothing nothing nothing nothing even on the mount nothing

The more I sought to have the less I possessed

neither this — nor this — nor this — nor this — nor this — nor this

How that I seek for nothing I have all without seeking

Way of imperfection with regard to earthly things: possession, joy, knowledge, consolation, rest

To attain to enjoyment of all things
desire to enjoy none
To attain to knowledge of all things
desire to know nothing of any
To attain to possession of all things
desire to possess none
To become everything
desire to be nothing

To reach that which you do not enjoy
you must travel by a way you do not enjoy
To reach that which you do not know
you must travel by a way you do not know
To attain to possession of what you have not
you must travel by a way you do not possess
To become what you are not
you must travel by a way in which you are not

When you linger over anything
you cease to cast yourself upon the All
because to pass from the all to the All
you must wholly renounce all
and when you have attained to all
you must rest it without desiring anything

In this nudity of spirit the
soul finds rest, for since it covers
nothing, nothing above lives it,
nothing below oppresses it, for it is
in the centre of its own humility

For my daughter Magdalen
Reproduction of the Original Sketch of Mount Carmel by St John of the Cross
unaltered apart from regularisation of the lines and translation of the Spanish and Latin words

Introduction

In December 1991 we celebrated the four hundredth anniversary of the death of John of the Cross. We cannot tell how much of his work was lost in the years immediately following his death. Precious letters and manuscripts were destroyed at that time for fear of the Spanish Inquisition, which was questioning his orthodoxy. Yet within a century and a half John was canonized as a saint, although two hundred years were to pass before he was proclaimed a doctor of the universal Church.

It would seem that the Church was in no hurry to give John this title, as if his teaching was not thought appropriate for the common mass of Christians. Even fifty years ago it was considered to be somewhat dangerous for the young. Yet John's own hope and intention was to help all those who were seeking God sincerely and with determination: "Our goal will be . . . that everyone who reads this book will in some way discover the road that he is walking along and the one he ought to follow if he wants to reach the summit of this Mount" (Prologue to *The Ascent of Mount Carmel*, 7). This does not mean that everything that he wrote is appropriate for everyone all the time, but that there is help for beginners as well as for the more advanced.

Today many people are attracted to John's writings through

the magic of his poetry, only to retire confused and repelled by the language and style of his prose works. For his wisdom is hidden within a theology, psychology and terminology which are not ours. There is a triple work of translation to be done if John's teaching is to make a practical impact on our lives today. We have the initial translation from Spanish to English in a variety of versions. But we also need a translation of the idiom of scholasticism into one which can be more readily understood by modern readers. Yet even this is not enough. Only through practice in daily living do we really come to know what it is all about. Carmelite spirituality, like anything else, can become an idol or a disembodied ideal unless it becomes a part of the fabric of our lives.

One of our legitimate difficulties on first meeting John of the Cross is that we may think him over-severe and anti-life. It is only as we penetrate more deeply that we find this is not so. He is uncompromising in his demands because he knows that God created the human heart for himself. Yet there is gentleness and moderation, common sense and humanity as well. He showed great tenderness toward the sick and poor both within and outside his community. Even if the attitude of a Brother left much to be desired, John would be patient until the offender was capable of hearing his rebuke. In contrast to many spiritual guides of his day, he disliked extravagant penances and practices. It was above all the desires and attitudes that needed to be directed Godward. His love was not of a rarified impersonal kind. He would introduce his brother Francesco to others with the words, "May I introduce you to my brother, who is the treasure I most value in the world?" Above all, in a life more than ordinarily marked by poverty, suffering and misunderstanding, he had learned to forgive. *The Spiritual Canticle*, written in his prison cell in Toledo, shows that nothing but the love of God remained in him.

Many scholars have written academic studies of John and

his writings, and without these our understanding of the saint would be impoverished. But these do not necessarily inspire us with a desire to take him for a spiritual guide. And John himself says that his way is one of love rather than intellect. Love can enter into his teaching through prayer and pondering on his texts. And love can draw the inner wisdom, which is applicable to every generation, out of the hard shell of a strange culture.

Our ways and degrees of loving are as unique as our genetic fingerprinting. Nevertheless we can believe that we all have a potential greater than we know, not because we are already holy but because we are human. God encourages us in our feeblest efforts. For our part we should not hold back through timidity or false humility, nor think that we have achieved our goal when we see far off some glimpses of the end.

We may feel that John's scheme is unnecessarily complicated, because he intended it to be comprehensive. In any case few of us are all that simple. For him a little reformation of the top layers of our life is only a beginning. He wants to open up the deep places where the unconscious but powerful desires and evasions are to be found. "For it is these which weary, torment, darken, defile and weaken the soul." He does not pretend that it is painless to bring them to the surface and surrender them into God's hands. Even our spiritual guides may prove a hindrance rather than a help. Yet, unless we are trying we cannot really help others or bring reconciliation to the area of the world for which we are responsible.

John was concerned not only with mystical prayer and the sanctification of the individual. His life was lived within the corporate rhythms of the Church's fasts and feasts. In his Toledo prison he was forbidden to celebrate the eucharist and this was his greatest deprivation. But as he shows in chapters xxxv-xlv of *Ascent* III, God is greater than all rites and aids. If we misuse them or are totally dependent on them they become idols.

In his daily life John's work was likewise not confined to purely spiritual matters. Apart from administrative and business concerns he would involve himself physically in any work that needed to be done. Whenever he had time he could be found helping with the chores, working in the garden and lending a hand with building and maintenance projects. He was in fact an exceptionally well-balanced man.

Although he spoke out of the Roman Catholic Church of sixteenth-century Spain, John's inner life was grounded in the spiritual heritage of the universal Church. Everything he wrote was based, either directly or indirectly, on holy scripture, and in this Protestants can identify with him. Likewise his teaching on the divinization of humanity is fundamental to Eastern Orthodoxy. The spirituality of the saints transcends time and religious culture, taking us back to our common roots. It can lead us to a vision of the Church which is far greater than the sum of its parts. Lacking this vision, the Church becomes fragmented and its missionary witness weak.

Translations

I have used the following translations of John's works:

Kieran Kavanaugh, O.C.D., and Otilio Rodriguez, O.C.D.,
   The Collected Works of St. John of the Cross
   (Washington DC: ICS Publications, 1973).
Kieran Kavanaugh, O.C.D. (ed.), *John of the Cross: Selected Writings,* The Classics of Western
   Spirituality (New York: Paulist Press, 1987).
John Venard, O.C.D., *The Spiritual Canticle: St. John of the Cross* (Newtown, Australia: E.J. Dwyer, 1980).

The Selected Writings gives a continuous flow to the line of John's thought but does not contain all the passages used here.

John Venard's simplified version of *The Spiritual Canticle* is very helpful and provides the foundation for my own comments on this book.

The section on intercession in chapter 4 of this book contains two quotations from a collection of Spiritual Sayings attributed to John of the Cross. These are taken from a document submitted by Fray Eliseo de los Martires (1550-1620), who was acquainted with the saint. The whole collection of seventeen Sayings can be found in the Appendices to *The Complete Works of St. John of the Cross*, translated and edited by E. Allison Peers. I have quoted from the sixth Saying.

References to particular passages of Saint John's writings are given at the head of the section which deals with them.

Finally let John's own words put us on the path of our pilgrimage:

> What do you ask then and seek, my soul? Yours is all of this and all is for you. Do not engage yourself on something less, nor pay heed to the crumbs which fall from your Father's table. Go forth and exult in your Glory! Hide yourself in it and you will obtain the supplications of your heart! ("Prayer of a Soul Taken with Love," in *Sayings of Light and Love*)

The life of John of the Cross

John of the Cross was born in 1542 at Fontiveros, a small town about twenty miles from Avila, Saint Teresa's birthplace. His father, Gonzalo de Yepes, came from a good family but was disowned when he married a poor silk-weaver, Catalina Alvarez. Gonzalo died when John was a small boy, leaving Catalina to rear John and his elder brother Francesco. She appealed for help to her husband's family but was rejected. Eventually she moved to Medina del Campo, the great market center for all Spain, where she hoped to be able to make a living by silk-weaving. Despite her courage and determination she could not earn enough for three. So she found for John a place in a school for poor and orphaned children where he could receive food and shelter, elementary education and training for a trade.

He did not find his right niche until the administrator of a local hospital saw his love for the poor and sick and offered him a post as a male nurse. Here he was in his element.

At the same time he began studying in the evenings at the Jesuit College in Medina and successfully completed the four-year course by the time he was twenty-one. Then he felt the call to the religious life. He asked to be admitted to the Carmelite Order and was accepted, spending a year at the monastery before going on to Salamanca University. After three years he was ordained as a priest in 1567 at the age of twenty-five.

John then returned to Medina del Campo and a few months later met Teresa, who had founded the first house of the Discalced Carmelite Reform at Saint Joseph's, Avila. She had also received permission from the head of the Order to found similar houses, following the strict observance of the Primitive Rule of Carmel, among the Carmelite friars. John had been looking for a stricter form of life, perhaps with the Carthusians, but Teresa persuaded him to join the Reform. First he returned to Salamanca University, where he took a year's course in theology, then he accompanied Teresa to Valladolid to be initiated into the customs and ways of the nuns there.

At last, in the autumn of 1568, John and two others set up the first Discalced Carmelite foundation for friars in a small farmhouse in the remote village of Duruelo. After eighteen months, the community, now numbering five members, moved to more spacious quarters at Pastrana, a hundred miles distant. From Pastrana a third foundation was made at Alcala, an important university city.

Then Teresa asked John to act as spiritual director to the

(unreformed) Convent of the Incarnation, where she had (with many misgivings) been appointed as superior. It was a large community with many problems. For five years—two of them alongside Teresa—John worked fruitfully among the nuns and the many others who sought his guidance. This aroused the jealousy of the unreformed Carmelites.

There is no need in this brief account to explore the bitter dispute which arose between the unreformed Calced Carmelites and the reformed Discalced who at this time were under the same jurisdiction. Sufficient to say that John was captured by his enemies in the Order, carried to Toledo and there imprisoned in a small, dark cell. During the nine months of his imprisonment he composed some of his most moving poems, including thirty-one stanzas of *The Spiritual Canticle*. One hot night in August 1578 John made his escape, taking refuge first of all with Teresa's nuns in Toledo and then at the nearby hospital of Santa Cruz. There he was restored to health and, after a meeting of the Discalced Superiors at Almodovar, sent to the remote monastery of El Calvario, where he would be in less danger of recapture.

At El Calvario John wrote the poem of *The Dark Night*, the *Sayings of Light and Love* and the prose commentary on them entitled *The Ascent of Mount Carmel*. It would have pleased John to remain in El Calvario, a place of great beauty, but other responsibilities were offered to him. He was appointed Rector of the College at Baeza, then Prior of the House and Third Definitor at Los Martires, Granada.

In 1580, through the personal intervention of King Philip II, the Discalced friars and nuns were allowed to form a separate province and govern themselves. In November 1581 John met Teresa for the last time. She died in October of the following year.

From 1582-88 John's home was in Granada with occasional visits to the nuns at Beas. During this time he wrote the last five stanzas of *The Spiritual Canticle* and the whole of the prose commentary on the poem. He also wrote the poem and commentary on *The Living Flame of Love*, the commentary on *The Dark Night* and poems and minor works. This was the most fruitful period of his life.

In 1585 John was made Vicar-General of Andalusia with charge of all the nuns' houses in that Province. Other responsibilities within the Order came his way. But toward the end of his life he fell into disfavor with the General of the Discalced Carmelites, Nicholas Doria. In 1591 he was deprived of his offices and the decision was taken, although afterward revoked, to send him to Mexico. Instead he went to the isolated monastery of Penuela. Attempts were made to banish him from the Order. At this time many of his letters and other writings were destroyed lest they should fall into the hands of the Inquisition. Since John's health was failing he was sent for medical attention to Ubeda. After ten weeks of great suffering he died on 14 December 1591 at the age of forty-nine.

He was beatified by Pope Clement X in 1675, canonized by Benedict XIII in 1736 and declared Doctor of the Universal Church by Pius XI in 1926.

On reading John

This book has been written for beginners who want to read the words of John of the Cross himself rather than accounts of his teaching by others. John encourages them to do this in his prologue to *The Ascent of Mount Carmel*:

> The reader should not be surprised if this doctrine on the dark night (through which a soul advances toward God) appears somewhat obscure. This I believe will be the case, but as he reads on he will understand it better since the latter parts will explain the former. Then if he reads this work a second time the matter will seem clearer and the doctrine sounder. (Prologue, 8)

John's works need to be read as one whole and to be read more than once if their full richness is to become available to the reader. However, John's undeniable obscurity may cause modern readers to question how or why they should proceed. In what order should his books be read? Are they meant only for "professionals" or are they applicable to all Christians? If so, how can the language and doctrine of scholasticism be relevant to the secular world of the twenty-first century? These and other questions may cause the prospective reader to look elsewhere for spiritual guidance or to read books about John rather than his actual words. This would be a pity, for the charisma and power of a spiritual teacher transmit themselves most fully through his or her own voice.

Nevertheless, the questions which have been mentioned need to be answered. That is the main purpose of the commentaries which accompany the selections from John's works in this book. These selections represent focal points around which further reading may be developed as desired.

The type of reading which John suggests is not that of academic criticism but rather of a spiritual reading which is close to prayer and open to everybody. In his prologue to *The Spiritual Canticle* he explains this to a Carmelite nun, Mother Anne of Jesus: "Even though Your Reverence lacks training in scholastic theology by which divine truths are understood, you are not wanting in mystical theology which is known through love and by which one not only knows but at the same time experiences" (#3). This knowledge depends on openness to the Holy Spirit and trust in the writer even when he speaks out of a strange culture and across the gulf of time. We need the ability to sort out universal truths from the packaging in which they are wrapped. In John's case there are three particular points among others which may confuse or irritate the beginner. These concern the nature of progression in the spiritual life; the relationship between divine and human love; and scholastic teaching on the make-up of the human person.

Progression

Nowadays we are uneasy with a system based on "ascension" or "progression" for we know from personal experience that the Holy Spirit is not bound by fixed laws. In the general movement of human beings toward God there are stages, but it may be that no two persons experience them exactly alike. Yet in the broadest sense there is inevitably a movement toward God or away from him, a choice between life and death which we make—often unconsciously—in every moment of our lives. John's aim is to describe the general way forward without laying down hard and fast rules. "It is better to explain the utterances of love in their broadest sense so that each one may derive profit from them according to the mode and capacity of his spirit rather than narrow them down to a meaning unadaptable to every palate" (Prologue to *The Spiritual Canticle*, 2).

Relationship between divine and human love

There are many passages in John's writings which at first sight seem to suggest that human loves are incompatible with love of God. Yet we believe that all true love comes from God as its sole source. For example, we are told that "Love effects a likeness between the lover and the object loved. . . . He who loves a creature then is as low as that creature and . . . even lower, because love not only equates, but even subjects the lover to the loved object" (*Ascent* I.iv.3). But here John is speaking of a possessiveness which cannot allow the desired object to be itself. However, we have to wait a long time before receiving a clear affirmation that real love of created beings and humanity is an essential part of our love for God. At the end of the journey,

God gathers together all the strength, faculties and appetites of the soul, spiritual and sensory alike, that the energy and power of this whole harmonious composite may be employed in this love. The soul consequently arrives at the true fulfillment of the first commandment *which neither disdaining anything human nor excluding it from this love* states: "You shall love your God with your whole heart and with your whole mind and with your whole soul and with all your strength." (*Night,* II.xi.4)

To this we should add John's great prayer from the *Sayings of Light and Love*: "Mine is the heaven and mine the earth." In this he affirms that all created beings are contained within his love for God.

The human person

Spiritual writers describe the make-up of the human person in a variety of ways, and we cannot understand them unless we enter their worlds while we are reading their works. Paul, for example, speaks of body, soul and spirit. John of the Cross, on the other hand, uses the definitions of scholastic philosophy in which he had been brought up. According to this scheme human beings contain within themselves a physical body and a soul. In the soul there are two parts, a sensual-soul which we share with the animal world and a higher spiritual-soul. In common with other animals we possess the senses of sight, hearing, touch, smell and taste. Like them we respond through these senses to stimuli coming from the outside world or to the pleasurable or painful memories that we have within us. We may shrink instinctively from a barking dog because long ago perhaps we were bitten by one. Likewise an animal may cringe at the sight of a stick, not because we have beaten it but because it remembers past maltreatment by somebody else. Animals have a form of memory, and some, such as dogs and monkeys, even possess a primitive emotional life. So we and they can be trained and conditioned through our actual senses or through what our senses remember.

However, unlike the animals, human beings have a spiritual-soul which contains more complex powers of understanding, memory and hope. Our joy, sorrow, hope and grief are centered around more solid and lasting sentiments, many of which are good and noble in themselves. We can include patriotism, religious culture, love of family or of a particular work for God among these ideals. Our inner life is colored through and through by the values of our particular culture. It is these which initially form our conscience. John would not deny their goodness, but at the top of his map of Mount Carmel are the words: "The honor and glory of God alone dwells on this Mount." We have to pass beyond our narrow insights and limitations if we want to be free. In that freedom we shall still thank God for the treasures of our own life and culture but see them in proportion, as our unique contribution to a whole which goes far beyond them.

In this spirit we can approach John's nights of sense and spirit positively. They are not meant to destroy us as persons but to set us free to be truly human. John did not have the insights of modern psychology, but in his own way he sorts out the truly spiritual from all the "soulishness" with which it is interwoven and through which it is expressed.

There is one final point. John is not at all consistent in his use of the words "soul" and "spirit." Sometimes we can only decide whether he is speaking of body-soul or spirit-soul or both through the context in which they appear. Yet we shall not go far astray if we keep in mind the unity of the human person who is never "nothing but body" or "nothing but soul" or "nothing but spirit." It is the whole organism which is created for God and his purposes in and for the world.

Prologue

Our Christian Calling

Cf. The Prologue to *The Ascent of Mount Carmel*

We have already seen in the Introduction that John's invitation to walk in the way of Mount Carmel is not limited to a few. None of us go through life without our experiences of night, and our growth as Christians depends on how we use them.

John says that these experiences are so profound and varied that holy scripture alone is capable of interpreting them. So he turns to the Bible continually, "at least in the most important matters and those which are difficult to understand" (Prologue, 2).

He encourages us not to be put off at the beginning by the obstacles that we shall encounter. Some of these will be due to ignorance and some to faintheartedness. A "Do It Yourself" attitude to prayer will not get us very far. Those who want to do everything for themselves "resemble children who kick and cry and strive to walk when their mothers want to carry them. Walking by themselves they make no headway or if they do it is at a child's pace" (Prologue, 3).

When we first come to know God in Jesus we want to hold on to the joy of that relationship. So when the sense of his presence fades we think that it is our own fault and that we just have to try harder. But according to John this is not the way forward. It is not by chance that an experience of joy and light is so often followed by one of desolation and a trial of faith. We need to learn how to walk upright through the night.

At the beginning we all kick and struggle against painful and humiliating experiences. But even if we succeed in banishing the darkness through our own ingenuity and willpower, a residue of pride and bitterness often remains. Or we may give up altogether, surrendering passively to what we believe to be the will of God. Yet this is a fatalistic rather than a Christian reaction. At this point we are not capable of judging God's intentions or his ways with us. It is better to seek below thought and feeling for that point where the umbilical cord between ourselves and our loving Lord still holds. In this confidence we are free to question God as the Jews in the Old Testament did frequently and vigorously. But let us not judge him too soon. Our nights may be a discipline, but they are certainly a challenge. God expects us to play up to him. So we try to accept ourselves and the situation as it is without self-pity or self-blame. Then the night begins to reveal the good things that lie hidden within it, things that we could never have guessed beforehand.

I remember having tea with a group of women and girls from the local Open Prison. They were mostly first offenders and one could guess what the trauma of their trials and imprisonment must have meant to them. It was therefore encouraging to hear of all that they had learned and done in prison, which otherwise would never have come their way. Some had passed their professional and technical examinations. They had learned to cook and paint and garden and even got themselves confirmed! And many were genuinely grateful for these opportunities. So in the end perhaps it does not really matter whether our suffering is due to our own fault or not, so long as we let something good grow out of it.

It is the same in the life of prayer. Prayer and life are two sides of the same coin, and John has already told us that our trials will be both "spiritual and temporal." Two obstacles in our inner life of prayer may be our own weakness and, possibly, unreliable guides. One great difficulty lies in our ignorance of where we are along the road and whether God is calling us to make some change in our life of prayer. On the one hand, we should not be too timid or set our sights too low:

> God gives *many* souls the talent and grace for advancing. . . . And so it is sad to see them continue their lowly form of communion with God because they do not want or know how to advance or because they receive no direction for breaking away from the methods of beginners. (Prologue, 3)

On the other hand our darkness and inability to pray may not be a call to a "higher" form of prayer but only to exercise patience and common sense where we are. Not everything in John's works is for everyone all the time, although there is always something for everyone. "With God's help then," says John, "we shall propose doctrine and counsel for beginners and proficients that they may understand or at least know how to practice abandonment to God's guidance when He wants them to advance" (Prologue, 4).

It would be helpful if our spiritual guides could show us the way ahead, but unfortunately they are not infallible.

> It will happen that while an individual is being conducted by God along a sublime path of dark contemplation and aridity in which he feels lost, he will encounter in the midst of the fullness of his darknesses, trials, conflicts and temptations someone . . . who will proclaim that all of this is due to melancholia or depression or temperament or to some hidden wickedness and that as a result God has forsaken him. (Prologue, 4)

This is not unknown today in some charismatic circles. But if we balance what we are told with prayerful reading of the Bible and the works of the great spiritual teachers of the universal Church, no one can lead us far astray.

From the prologue we can carry away the thought of human potential. You and I are called to nothing less than participation in the life of God. Something of this can be known even in our earthly existence. Why then is our progress so slow? Why don't more of us get further on our way? When the Son of God came to earth he used the circumstances that he found; we must do the same. Essentially, it is not the amount of time and solitude that we have for prayer that counts, although we all need what we can get. John himself did not sit all day long with folded hands in contemplation. He was not only a poet and a theologian but also a reformer and an administrator. He had known poverty from his earliest youth and knew what it was to work with his hands. Everything that happens to us, everyone we meet can be a gateway to God if we are open and listening for his message coming in and through them. Otherwise circumstances become a prison no matter how gilded the cage may be.

> If I climb the heavens, You are there,
> If I lie in the grave, You are there,
>   If I take the wings of the dawn
> and dwell at the sea's farthest end,
>   even there Your hand would lead me
>   Your right hand would hold me fast.
>
>   (Psalm 139:8-10)

Meeting Saint John Today

The Dark Night

1. One dark night,
   Fired with love's urgent longings
        —Ah, the sheer grace!—
   I went out unseen,
   My house being now all stilled;

2. In darkness and secure,
   By the secret ladder, disguised,
        —Ah, the sheer grace!—
   In darkness and concealment,
   My house being now all stilled;

3. On that glad night,
   In secret, for no one saw me,
   Nor did I look at anything,
   With no other light or guide
   Than the one that burned in my heart;

4. This guided me
   More surely than the light of noon
   To where He waited for me
        —Him I knew so well—
   In a place where no one else appeared.

5. O guiding night!
    O night more lovely than the dawn!
    O night that has united
    The Lover with His beloved,
    Transforming the beloved in her Lover.

Meeting the poet

Cf. The first eight in the collected poems:
> The Dark Night
> The Spiritual Canticle (1st Redaction)
> The Living Flame of Love
> "I entered into unknowing"
> "I live but not in myself"
> "I went out seeking love"
> "A lone young shepherd"
> "For I know well the spring"

After reading these poems we can have no doubt that we are in the presence of someone who loves God and knows that he is loved. Some people may find John's language too extravagant, but it is not more so than that of the Song of Songs in the Old Testament. In both cases the language of earthly love is used to describe the meeting of humanity with God, for it does not refer only to the individual relationship. In John's poem on the lone young shepherd, the shepherd-girl for whom he dies could represent the Church, you or me, or the whole of humanity. This is one reason why John's poems are not pietistic or sentimental. There was no room for sentiment in the dark and narrow cell in the Toledo prison where some of his most moving poems were written. On the human side there was nothing but loneliness and suffering; in the poetry, however, this is transformed. Suffering has become the raw material for glory and darkness more illuminating than light.

In the poems we find a whole range of meaning contained

in John's image of night. Not all of it is painful, for there is joy and discovery on the way as well as suffering. However, as one would expect, there are a number of references to the darkness of God's apparent absence:

Where have you hidden
Beloved and left me moaning?
. . . I went out calling you and
You were gone.

(The Spiritual Canticle, 1)

We shall experience the night of pain which is inseparable from love.

Why, since you wounded
This heart, don't you heal it?

(Canticle, 9)

The intellect alone is not capable of understanding the mysteries of God:

The higher he ascends
The less he understands
Because the cloud is dark
Which lit up the night.

("I entered into unknowing," 5)

God conceals and also reveals himself in the mystery of the eucharist:

This eternal spring is hidden
In this living bread for our life's sake
Although it is night.

("For I know well the spring," 9)

And finally there is the night of union.

O night more lovely than the dawn!
O night that has united
The lover with His beloved
Transforming the beloved in her Lover.

(*The Dark Night*, 5)

Within these poems we shall find the primal vision which inspired John's major prose works: *The Ascent of Mount Carmel, The Dark Night of the Soul, The Spiritual Canticle* and *The Living Flame of Love.* We shall consider these in more detail later. For the present let us look at the imagery he uses.

The basic image is a simple one. God, the Bridegroom, calls in the night to the Bride, not for any virtue of her own but out of "sheer grace." She goes out of her house, by way of the secret stair into the unknown, guided only by the light of her love. In that night she finds the Lover in a place known only to the two of them. For this meeting is unique and special for every person. "I will give to them a white stone on which is written a new name that no one knows except the one who receives it" (Rev 2:17).

The commentaries on *The Dark Night* and *The Ascent* are mainly concerned with the difficulties and challenges involved in leaving our safe and familiar "houses" to follow God's call.

In *The Spiritual Canticle* this stage is summarized in the Introduction. John is more concerned here with the actual journey which will ultimately bring the soul into complete union with God. We may sense his presence first of all in the beauties and wonders of nature, but these will soon pall. "Do not send me any more messengers. They cannot tell me what I must hear" (*Canticle*, 6). It is prayer and obedience to his word which will bring us closer to him. John calls this stage the "spiritual espousals." We are committed to God, but many things will attack or weaken or unsettle us. He uses a variety of images to describe these enemies of the soul. They include the "little foxes" (*Canticle*, 25), "the deadening North wind" (*Canticle*, 26), "the girls of Judea" (*Canticle*, 31), "the swift-winged birds" and "the watching fears of night" (*Canticle*, 29). But as love grows stronger these have less power over us. We become more Christ-like and therefore more at one with the God of love. John speaks of this as the spiritual marriage, which can be experienced partially in this life but in completion only in the life to come.

The Living Flame of Love is based on a line from stanza 38 of *The Canticle*: "With a flame that is consuming and painless." In this book John describes, as best as he can, the life of transformation. Many of us may catch a glimpse of what this poem is saying to our spirits long before the burning edge of its reality penetrates our lives.

It is true that our marriage with God, like earthly marriages, is not all rapture, and has to be worked out in the nitty-gritty of life as it is. Yet without the poetry, and the passion which inspires it, we would be left only with a set of religious and moral rules rather than the adventure of life in Christ which Christianity is meant to be.

Original vision

In these poems John shares with us something of his love and search for God. Yet, however moving his witness may be, we can only participate in his vision second hand. Have we no vision of our own?

The Alastair Hardy Research Center in Oxford, England, which explores the nature and incidence of religious experience, believes that many (if not all) of us do receive some primal vision in our early life. Our capacity to accept and respond is a part of our human potential. In childhood such experiences are received simply, without self-consciousness or exaggeration. They are rarely spoken of at the time, but they are not forgotten. At the time of writing, the Center has already collected over five thousand testimonies from people in all walks of life. Their experiences were triggered off in a variety of ways: through nature, through liturgy, through reading a particular book, through mathematics or music. Yet they have certain things in common. They are unforgettable and have colored the person's entire later life. They have given an understanding of the unity of all life and of the individual's place within it. There has been a sense of something mysterious, good and beautiful penetrating into the homeliness of things around. An affinity is felt with people, plants and animals, which can be the foundation of compassionate understanding in later life.

We can guess that the reading of the Song of Songs in the Old Testament was John's sparking-off point. But that was only the beginning of a vision which he developed and understood through a lifetime of experience and suffering. For although these moments may influence our future life, they do not add up to much unless they are used as a foundation for a fully Christian faith.

The inner faith-story of a Christian may develop in an infinite variety of ways. Yet each experience contains within it the seed of the next. Gradually and slowly, often with many set-backs and false starts, the whole of the person is drawn into obedience to the indwelling Christ and through him to union with God.

So one young woman writes:

My first moments of religious experience came when I was six or seven years old. I used to take my Children's Encyclopedia into the garden on starry nights to look at the constellations and try to name them. It was almost incidental that I became aware of a Presence surrounding and supporting me in a love and reassurance which was somehow different from the love of my parents.

This is a typical religious experience but not necessarily a Christian one. The next memory dates from a year or two later.

I began to clamor to go to Matins in place of Sunday School which my parents thought much more suitable. Although I could not tell them, the secret attraction was the *Te Deum*. I had seen the pictures of the apostles, martyrs, prophets and confessors in the stained glass windows. Now, in the music they became alive, both as a company of friends and as a part of that hidden Presence that I had experienced in the night.

Here the original vision is taken into the life of the Church, it is no longer seen only as a solitary experience; the communion of saints is recognized as a reality.

Years of adolescence followed in which the original child's vision began to focus itself into the form of Jesus.

At the time of my confirmation Jesus became alive for me as a person. I felt his presence within me, even though, soon after, I abandoned church services for several years. For as I read the Bible in the vaguely fundamentalist way which was all that I knew, I found that there was a lot that I couldn't take. Being adolescent, honesty demanded a visible protest! However, I remember my relief when eventually I was introduced to modern biblical theology and realized that, although it did not have all the answers, it made belief possible.

If we continued this story we should see the gradual weaving in of the other elements that form the Christian life. We should see the struggle to fulfill its ethical demands, to relate to others, to react to life in faith, hope and charity. It is a lifetime's program and the main subject of John's teaching, especially in *The Ascent of Mount Carmel* and *The Dark Night of the Soul*.

Some will say that their Christian vision has come to them in very different ways. They may have found Christ wholly through other people, or through some great sense of release from guilt and sin. God has his own way for each of us. All of us rely on others for support and growth; all of us have sinned and need repentance. But happy are they who in the dawn of life experience touches of God's beauty and love. For when the troubles and responsibilities of life threaten to overwhelm them they will not easily judge God nor lose their faith in him.

John's last request as he lay on his death-bed was for verses from the Song of Songs to be read to him. "O que preciosas margaritas!" he murmured, "What precious pearls!" Shortly afterward he died. So the vision which had accompanied him throughout his hard life sustained him still as he passed through the gates of death into the life beyond. May it be so with us.

The Dark Night

Cf. *The Ascent of Mount Carmel* I.i; ii.1; iii.1; iv

We looked first at the positive side of John's teaching in order to avoid a distorted impression of his nights. But the two aspects must be held together if we are to understand his doctrine as one whole.

We have already seen in his poems that John's image of night is a complex one, and he elaborates this in the first verse of *Ascent*, I.ii. There are three reasons for calling the journey toward union with God a night. The world at night can appear a strange and frightening place, as we are deprived of the sight of familiar scenes and landmarks. When we enter our inner world we experience privation there too, as well-worn attitudes and possessions no longer seem appropriate. A sense of deprivation is one aspect of night.

Secondly, the road itself is invisible in the dark. We cannot see the obstacles and turns on the way, but we trust that it will ultimately lead us to our goal. In the spiritual world the name of the path is faith. It can lead us into situations which our critical intellect would prefer to reject, but it is our only valid way forward. So John says that for the intellect, faith resembles a dark night.

Thirdly, by night the destination also is shrouded in darkness. This is so with us, as we move toward union with a God whom we cannot see in this life. God himself is a dark night in which we can only experience glimpses of his reality.

Yet this darkening is a necessary element of growth. "These three nights pass through the soul, or better the soul passes through them in order to reach divine union with God" (*Ascent*, I.ii.1).

The subject of the first book of *The Ascent* is our departure from those inner "houses" in which we have been imprisoned by our desires and attachments. For these houses contain many treasured possessions which may have to be left behind if we want to draw nearer to God. They may be centered on bodily comforts such as food and drink, or the comfort, companionship and approval of our fellow human beings, or consoling prayer and uplift in worship. We may be asked to leave them only for a while. On the other hand the deprivation may last for a lifetime. We cannot find our freedom to give ourselves to God except by some token of denial of our lesser gods. We can tell what these are and the degree of their power over us by the amount of irritation, anger or depression that we feel when we are deprived of them.

At the end of the Introduction to this book we explained how scholastic philosophy analyzed the human person as a living organism. With this in mind let us look at John's program of training for the soul.

> The first night or purgation . . . concerns the sensory part of man's nature. The second stanza refers to the night of the spiritual part of man's soul. . . . The first night is the lot of beginners. . . . The second night or purification takes place in those who are already proficients at the time God desires to lead them into the state of divine union. (*Ascent*, I.i.2 and 3)

We may not like the cut and dried nature of a scheme based on progression. Yet in his own way John understands that human beings operate as one entity, with every part affecting the rest. The first night of the senses may be the lot of beginners, but "it is a night in which the spirit of man also participates" (*Ascent*, I.i.3).

In John's scheme the essential goodness of human nature in its potential for glory is taken for granted. Nevertheless, this goodness is tarnished and its sense of direction distorted by the multitude of lesser desires which wage war against it. Physical and sensual attachments are on the whole closest to the surface. But as we try to let go of these things we begin to discover the hidden depths where our most intimate loves, fears and prejudices have their being. These often contain much that is good, but they can easily become idols if they are not subordinated to the greater glory of God.

John tells us that we shall experience the "nighting" of sense and spirit in two ways. In the active nights there is something that we can do through our own efforts, aided by the grace and call of God. But these are interspersed with passive states into which God himself puts us, often against our own will. Here we can do nothing but remain as still and patient as we can, and let him do the work. This is often more difficult than trying to do everything ourselves.

In *Ascent*, I.iv John sets our idols against the glory of our end. But we may feel that the journey is long and difficult and that our familiar compensations did at any rate help us to get through it. So it is not surprising that it may take much struggle and pain before our inner houses are really still. We may feel that we were much nicer people to know when we were drugging ourselves with coffee, TV, cigarettes, or whatever our favorite dope may have been. These things are not necessarily bad in themselves. As John says, "Since the things of the world cannot enter the soul, they are not in themselves an encumbrance or harm to it; rather, it is the will and appetite dwelling within it that causes the damage" (*Ascent*, I.iii.4). For instance, many of us have to take drugs and other medical aids as our bodies age and begin to wear out. And where would we be without them! So this is not wrong unless our lives become obsessed with health and medical treatment. For this dependence has reason behind it; it is not a way of escaping from reality.

We may still be asking ourselves whether John's nights are applicable to us today. Aren't we a different breed, needing other ways of finding God and being found by him? We need to consider this question before embarking on a quest which eventually will ask not less than everything.

Night in the world today

The world of post-Renaissance Spain was in many ways different from ours. It was self-confident, wealthy and apparently secure. It had no wide world-view to disturb its complacency. Spanish galleons were bringing their treasures from the New World in ever-increasing quantities, although little of this found its way to the poor and needy. For others everything seemed possible. Close behind the explorers came the missionaries bringing the Catholic faith and Spanish culture.

The spirit of the age was expressed in the baroque art of the period. We marvel today at the churches of Spain and Austria which were built at this time. They seem to us to be like religious opera houses for the performance of the divine liturgy. Fat cherubs, statues of rapturous saints, the lavish use of gold leaf and elaborate music all contributed to the richness and exaggeration which John had to accept publicly but deplored in his inner heart.

Our world is a more ramshackle place. The media ensure that nothing in religion, politics or society goes unquestioned. Strikes and protests are part of our everyday life as they could never have been in John's time. We are left with few of the certainties of his generation. It is true that English pirates on the high seas and Lutheran heretics over the border were disturbing their security. The world was gradually changing but not at the speed that we are experiencing in the present century.

Yet the souls that go out from such different houses in search of God have much in common, although one building may appear to be solid and well-built and the other ready to collapse at any moment. We are haunted by the fear that we shall destroy our world; John's contemporaries feared the destruction of the Last Judgement and the pains of hell. The poor are still with us as they were then, dependent on charity and knowing the humiliation that goes with it. Our safety net is the Welfare State and voluntary agencies; theirs was a paternalistic Church. Divorce was unknown in Catholic Spain, but John himself was from an early age the child of a one-parent family. He knew the deprivation of the fatherless, like many others at a time when life was short and precarious. We know, at least at second hand, the fear of those who suffer under totalitarian regimes. But John lived his life under the shadow of the Inquisition, which would probably have destroyed him had he lived longer.

So the afflictions and perils that threaten the individual do not greatly vary from one generation to another. We all know the inner insecurity which makes us cling to things that must pass away. We also know the greed and pride that tempt us to fill our "houses" with things we do not really want or need, often at the expense of others. But human nature moved by God is also capable of courage, compassion and integrity. Deep within us we have the capacity to reject the lesser for the greater and more lasting goals.

Modern psychology has complicated matters for us. We wonder if its insights have made John's teaching out of date and even harmful to people today. When we are confronted by our disordered and conflicting desires we are tempted to think that this may be so. Often our understanding of the workings of our psychology is very imperfect, and we confuse self-control with repression. We identify ourselves with the inner mess and not with our potential, so that in denying ourselves in outward ways we feel that we are being hypocritical and acting a part which is untrue to reality. But God in Jesus is the inmost reality of our human nature. If we do not deny or suppress the existence of the mess but lay it open to him, we may hope to receive ongoing help and encouragement from the other side.

Psychological insights can help the soul to learn the art of loving. Psychotherapy may result in a greater capacity for self-respect and acceptance of all aspects of ourselves. John wants this too, as he begs us to consider the greatness of the calling for which we were created. Properly understood, the nights have the power to heal our wounded personalities, enabling them to become truly human as Jesus was. Therapists encourage their clients to adjust to reality. For John, too, our environment and circumstances, just as they are, provide the background and substance of our nights. He offers no escape into a fairy-tale world of our own choosing in which all the conditions are ideal, for few of us have the opportunity to manipulate our outward situations. Healing has to happen where we are or not at all.

In the end, psychotherapy, if successful, will have given the client a greater capacity for love, although not necessarily love for God. In this respect psychology is limited. For medicine and psychology are sciences of the human person. Mystical theology is concerned with God in his relationship to humanity and the rest of the created world. It teaches us the art of giving ourselves over to him. But we cannot do this or respond positively to the nights unless and until we have a self which is capable of love. So psychology and mystical theology, rightly understood and practiced, do not threaten but complement each other. Analysis becomes sterile if in the process we become so self-absorbed that we are no longer capable of hearing the Spirit's voice when he speaks to us through other means.

Ultimately, the soul that loves God will have no need of psychological supports. They will be left behind in the gift of the total self to God. Because he encompasses all times and all places, this possibility is open to all who try to center their wills on him. John's language and imagery may not always appeal to us, but the broad principles that he teaches cannot alter from generation to generation, because loss of the false self in order to find one's true humanity is at the heart of the Christian experience.

The Map of Mount Carmel

Cf.   The sketch-map of Mount Carmel drawn by John of the Cross
       Stanza 3 of *The Spiritual Canticle* with
          its commentary (2d redaction)

We shall find John's map at the beginning of his book on *The Ascent of Mount Carmel* (see page 10 in the present book). When he drew it he saw, in his mind's eye, Mount Carmel in Israel, which gave its name to the Carmelite Order to which he belonged. Centuries before, Christian hermits had lived on the slopes of this mountain until driven out by Saracen invaders. Since then they had made their home in western Europe. So Mount Carmel was always a holy place in the minds and memories of Carmelites. When John was explaining the spiritual way, it was not surprising that he used a sketch-map of this mountain as an illustration, or that he gave copies of it to his spiritual children. An original drawing remains, addressed "To my daughter Magdalen."

The map shows a roughly-drawn hill with three paths going up it. The middle path goes straight up the mountain, and even in the sketch we can guess that it is steep. "Nothing, nothing, nothing, and even on the Mount nothing" is written all the way up. Yet it opens out into a rich place. Here we find the words: "I brought you into the land of Carmel to eat of its fruit and good things" (Jer 2:7). "Only the honor and glory of God dwells on this Mount." Dotted around are the names of the good things to be found there, such as peace, joy, happiness, justice, wisdom, strength and love. At the summit of the mountain there is nothing left but the law of love. "Here there is no longer any way because for the just man there is no law, he is a law unto himself."

But John also draws attention to two other paths, one going to the right and the other to the left, climbing up into the mountain but stopping far short of the top. The right-hand path is marked "The way of the imperfect spirit in goods of earth" and the left-hand route "The way of the imperfect spirit in goods of heaven." These contrast with the middle road, "The path of Mount Carmel, the perfect spirit." Written on the path of earthly goods are the words "The more I desired to *seek* them the less I had," and on the path of heavenly goods, "The more I desired to *possess* them the less I had." On these paths we are still Christians, even if imperfect ones. All of us stray from the center from time to time, more often through weakness than deliberate sin. Our progress is marked by the speed of our return. So we are always repentant sinners before God, rather than supermen and superwomen who never go wrong.

For the moment we will leave the verses written at the base of the map and return to them later.

As we have already seen, it is our attitude of mind toward all possessions that counts rather than the things themselves. John's map shows that we are in danger whenever we seek "glory, joy, knowledge, consolation and rest" in any attitude or habit which dilutes our dependence on Christ. Earthly goods include necessities as well as luxuries, but still we have to sit lightly on them. My mother used to say to her whining child, "The more you have, the more you want." This attitude of never-satisfied desire yields fewer and poorer results the more we give in to it.

To desire heavenly goods seems at first sight to be more praiseworthy, but not in John's eyes. To cling to little bits of spiritual insight or emotional sweetness which we have received in the past, holds up our progress in the present. So does over-dependence on exterior forms of worship, aids to prayer, talented preachers, holy places or any other spiritual good which comes to be more important to us than our allegiance to Christ.

John must have had this map in mind when he wrote stanza 3 of *The Spiritual Canticle*:

> Seeking my Love
> I will head for the mountains and the watersides,
> I will not gather flowers, nor fear wild beasts;
> I will go beyond strong men and frontiers.

Each of these images represents some aspect of Christian experience. Heading for the mountains symbolizes the efforts that we make in the active nights. The watersides are the places where we learn to accept the frailty and feebleness of our human condition. The flowers by the wayside are the attractions and enticements of the world. The wild beasts represent its threatening and demanding aspects. (Apparently even in sixteenth-century Catholic Spain one could risk loss of friends, reputation and importance through being thought too religious.) The strong men are the devils or powers of evil, which take advantage of our weakness, while the frontiers which we have to pass are the rebellions of the flesh against the spirit.

We shall never be free from temptation in one form or another, but right from the beginning we need to form habits of turning to God after any fall or looking through the temptation to him. Such habits will be formed not through the occasional grand gesture but in the opportunities of daily life, which may seem too trivial and banal to be taken into account. Yet it is through these that the battle will be lost or won, as the following example will show.

In preparation for half an hour of prayer I have switched on the answering machine so that no one can disturb me. Yet scarcely have I settled down when the anxious face of my cat appears at the window. She wants to be let in, but this would only be the beginning of her demands. So I pull a curtain across the window, shutting her out. This is difficult. I love my cat, but I am not her slave! I settle down into prayer only to be disturbed perhaps by sudden inner temptations. When I am feeling nearest to God I may be shaken by violent tempests of anger, depression or lust, which seem to have no definite cause. They may come from the powers of evil or, more likely, from my own as yet unhealed unconscious. In either case I need to be kind to myself, not making matters worse with self-reproach or analysis. It is better to ride out the storm looking through it to God and his all-embracing love. Finally, after all this effort I may feel the need for refreshment, which nevertheless can wait quite well until the allotted time for prayer is completed.

We may wonder where prayer comes into all this. Yet I have made four separate decisions for God, like four stepping-stones up the mountain. However feeble the rest of my prayer may have been, these decisions were prayer. Sometimes it is true that we have to leave God in order to find him in some duty or emergency. But unless and until we have built up habits of putting God first in our lives, we shall hardly be capable of discerning between a good reason and an excuse. John sums up the journey in a few words.

> The method, in sum, consists in steadfastness and courage in not stopping to gather flowers; of bravery in not fearing the wild beasts, of strength in passing by strong men and frontiers; and of the sole intention to head for the mountains and watersides of virtues. (*Canticle*, Commentary on Stanza 3.10)

In the course of time other artists re-drew John's map, making it more elaborate. Sometimes the side-paths were made to disappear outside the mountain as if there could be no salvation for the imperfect. John, on the other hand, shows that somewhere on his holy mountain there is room for all. Yet he also makes it plain that only wholehearted lovers will be given the full freedom of the high places of Mount Carmel.

2

The Active Night of Sense

Detachment

Cf. *Ascent*, I.vi.1; xi; xii.6

It is regrettable, then, to behold some souls, laden as rich vessels with wealth, deeds, spiritual exercises, virtues and favors from God, never advancing because they lack the courage to make a complete break with some little satisfaction, attachment, or affection (which are all about the same), and thereby never reaching the port of perfection, which requires no more than a sudden flap of one's wings to tear the thread of attachment. . . . It is a matter for deep sorrow that, while God has bestowed on them the power to break other stronger cords of attachment to sins and vanities, they fail to attain so much good because they do not become detached from some childish thing which God has requested them to conquer out of love for Him and which amounts to no more than a thread or hair. (*Ascent*, I.xi. 4 and 5)

In the first book of *The Ascent* John discusses the active night of sense as it concerns the right-hand bypath of the "way of the imperfect spirit in the goods of earth." As he says,

We are not discussing mere lack of things; this lack will not divest the soul if it craves for all these objects. We are dealing with the denudation of the soul's appetites and gratifications; this is what leaves it free and empty of all things even though it possesses them. (*Ascent,* I.iii.4)

People of any or no religion may give up certain earthly pleasures for the sake of health or the environment or for the world's poor. Praiseworthy though it may be to renounce cigarettes, alcohol, clothes made from animal fur, or meat products, this alone will not bring us into the night of sense. In fact if we become self-righteous and critical as a result of our self-denial we may be further from God than before.

John's concern is with something different. He knows that when the first joy of commitment to Christ begins to fade and his presence becomes less clear, previous attachments of various kinds will again rear their heads. Some may be very small. In chapter xi.4 John gives examples: a need to chatter incessantly, small attachments to a person, to clothing, to a book, a room, the way food is prepared, to little satisfactions in tasting, knowing and hearing things. There may also be greater attachments which involve us in one or other of the seven principal sins. These will separate us from God in a way that little imperfections will not.

It makes little difference whether a bird is tied by a thin thread or by a cord. For even if tied by thread, the bird will be prevented from taking off just as surely as if it were tied by cord—that is, it will be impeded from flight as long as it does not break the thread. (*Ascent,* I.xi.4)

These small harmful attachments may help us to get through life for a while but eventually, John says, "the sour effect is felt." The unsatisfied cravings that we feel weary, torment, darken, defile and weaken the soul. In chapters vi-x John examines each of these effects in turn. Our souls, he says, grow weary in battling for our own way, are tormented by fears and suspicions that our toys are going to be taken from us. Our minds become darkened and defiled so that we can no longer see things objectively, nor distinguish good from evil. We judge from our own blinded viewpoint. Finally we are weakened both as human beings and as Christians so that we are not the persons that God intends us to be. But he does not normally free us without some action, however small, on our part. John tells us that a person "must not give the consent of his will knowingly to an imperfection, and he must have the power and freedom to be able, upon advertence, to refuse this consent" (*Ascent*, I.xi.3).

John is concerned only about attachments which take away our freedom. He is not referring to the natural, God-given appetites which enable us to cope with our human needs and relate to our environment and to other people.

> The natural ones are little or no hindrance at all to the attainment of union, provided they do not receive one's consent nor pass beyond the first movements in which the rational will plays no role. For to eradicate the natural appetites . . . is impossible in this life. (*Ascent*, I.xi.2)

Even when our wills are united to God in prayer, our senses may be running round like squirrels in a cage. Yet they can do no harm if we keep returning to God and pay no attention to them.

Let us consider, for instance, the part played by natural, semi-voluntary and obsessive desires in our attitude to food. God has given us sight, smell and taste-buds to enable us to enjoy our meals. Therefore we can believe that he likes to see us doing it. Yet there is a time and a place for everything. We all know how a sudden urge for food or drink may afflict us even in the midst of important work or prayer. John would call this a "semi-voluntary" desire which should be resisted. He says that usually this does not present a problem even though we may be left with a residue of irritation or depression. This does not defile the soul. However, obsessive attachments to food and drink are the real danger. Even though they may be symptomatic of something deeper, even though we cannot tell why we act as we do, there is a need to cut off the symptoms as a first step toward our healing. We do this, John says, in the darkness of faith, and in the measure in which we persevere we find freedom to give ourselves more wholly to God.

Obviously we need self-knowledge, but this cannot be obtained by delving unaided into the morass of our hearts and minds. We are too close to ourselves and too involved to see straight. John would expect everyone to have a spiritual guide or soul-friend to help the soul know itself. Good guides were not easy to find even in his uncomplicated age. The problem is no easier today. We may be helped to understand our strengths and weaknesses through the many aids to self-awareness which are available to us today. But in every human being there is an area of mystery which does not fit into a type and is known only to God.

So John's solution lies in looking away from ourselves to Jesus, who is the fullness of our humanity; for, as he says, we become like the thing we love.

Entering in

Cf. *Ascent*, I.xiii.1-4

This reference is short, because John has little to say about the manner in which "we should study Christ's life in order to imitate Him." There is only one passage in his works in which he describes the methods of active meditation.

> For a better understanding of this beginners' stage, it should be known that the practice of beginners is to meditate and make acts and discursive reflection with the imagination. A person in this state should be given matter for meditation and discursive reflection, and he should by himself make interior acts and profit in spiritual things from the delight and satisfaction of his senses. For being fed with the relish of spiritual things, the appetite is torn away from sensual things and weakened in regard to the things of the world." (*The Living Flame of Love*, stanza 3.32)

The aim of this form of meditation is to help us to know Jesus as a living person whose image is strong enough to wean us from absorption in ourselves. At this stage the senses are to be encouraged to play their part. We are accustomed to using them in all the affairs of daily life. Now they are to be employed in building up our image of God in Christ Jesus.

This type of meditation was as popular in John's day as it is in ours. It was associated with Ignatius of Loyola and the Jesuit Order, and as John was a student at the Jesuit College in Medina del Campo for four years, he would have practiced this form of prayer himself.

In Ignatian meditation the senses of sight, hearing, touch, taste and smell are used through our powers of fantasy and imagination. Through fantasy we form pictures in our mind; through imagination we ponder upon them. Our prayer develops out of these two exercises. We begin by reading a gospel passage. Then the senses are used to form as vivid a picture as possible of the scene of the story. For instance, if we take Luke 8:22-25, which tells of Christ stilling the storm, we would first try to see before us a lake that we have seen and known (if we have never actually visited the Sea of Galilee). Through our memory we re-create the surroundings, weather, colors and scents of the landscape and listen to the lapping of the waves and other sounds. We look at the actors in the scene, Jesus, the disciples and the spectators and ask ourselves what they would be thinking, feeling and saying. We ourselves become involved, talking to Jesus about the passage we have read, listening to his reply, and noting our own feelings and responses. Then we come to a moment of choice. Jesus is asking something of us. Are we ready to give it? Do we believe that his words have power to change us? We have to make some response even though it may be one of sadness and anger that we cannot yet reply with a wholehearted "Yes." At the end we spend a while resting in his presence, not thinking or working but being quiet for as long as we can.

John himself does not go into such detail because, as we have seen, he would expect everyone to have a spiritual guide who would show them how to proceed. Today many people take guided or one-to-one retreats in order to get the help which they cannot find elsewhere.

John recognizes that this form of meditation is hard work. If our time for prayer has to be short or we become exhausted, it can be spread over several days and lived with in free moments in between. John points out that the whole aim of the exercise is to gain more knowledge and love of God. We do this through the acts and prayers that we make in the course of our meditation. The essential thing is that such prayer, whether long or short, should become a habit and a part of life. "Many acts, in no matter what area, will engender a habit. Similarly, the repetition of many particular acts of this loving knowledge becomes so continuous that a habit is formed in the soul" (*Ascent* II.xiv.2).

We believe that as time goes on our prayer will become more simple and direct, but unless it is grounded in the work of meditation we may find that we are talking not to God but to ourselves. We must look to Jesus in his incarnate life, as he is shown to us in the gospels. Then we shall be ready to seek him alive in the depths of our souls.

Breaking the bonds

Cf. *Ascent*, I.xiii. 5-11

> Endeavor to be inclined always,
> ·   not to the easiest, but to the most difficult;
>   not to the most delightful, but to the harshest;
>   not to the most gratifying, but to the less pleasant;
>   not to what means rest for you, but to hard work;
>   not to the consoling, but to the unconsoling;
>   not to the most, but to the least. . .
>   not to be wanting something, but to be wanting
>   nothing.

(*Ascent*, I.xiii.6)

So the passage continues in a similar vein. It is one which may repel modern readers. Deep down we feel that our relationship with God cannot be improved by our own self-conscious acts of virtue. It is his love alone which can embrace the mess that we are, and in doing so save and redeem it. This is so, but true salvation brings with it a desire to be more like the one who has accepted us. To grow up in love involves struggle and expansion. Popular psychology may try to persuade us that it is sick to be inclined toward the unpleasant, difficult and apparently unrewarding things of life, rather than those which boost us as persons. Yet we do not deny the need for hardship and discipline in some areas of secular life. The sportsman, the Arctic or space explorer, the business person, the medical researcher can all benefit from practicing at least some of John's maxims. However, when it comes to personal relationships with God and human beings we are tempted to feel that such methods are masochistic and anti-life.

Perhaps the language of story and parable may be more acceptable to us than moral precepts. As Jesus himself showed, parable is the language of the religious spirit. Stories which have survived the years have done so because we feel in our hearts that they are saying something true about our human condition.

One such story is that of Beauty and the Beast. The Beast seems in her eyes to be all that is strange, difficult, humiliating, unpleasant and undesirable. Beauty is attractive, as young love can be, but her judgements are narrow and shallow and her capacity for love is small. It is only when she brings herself to embrace the Beast that he shows himself in his true light as the prince of her dreams. In union with him her horizons widen, her values change and she becomes more lovable herself.

So John leads us gently on to our meeting place with those things that we find most difficult to accept. Unlike the sportsman, the explorer or the medical researcher, we cannot have a clearly defined goal before us. In "nudity, emptiness and poverty" we go forward in hope that the Beast will turn into the prince as we embrace him. Christ often comes to us in the unknown guise of the Beast, so that we do not know who it is that we are accepting or rejecting. In the end we shall find delight and consolation in what we used to abhor because we will have changed.

The words at the base of the map of Mount Carmel were taken up by T. S. Eliot in his poem *East Coker*. But the truth they express may be found in an earlier piece of literature. In Lewis Carroll's book *Alice Through the Looking-Glass* Alice tries again and again to enter a beautiful garden but each time finds herself farther away from the entrance. Then she is told to go in the opposite direction. Ridiculous advice she thinks, but she follows it. Soon she finds herself walking in the garden among the flowers, the creatures and the sweet scents. This episode is a parable of detachment. If we go all out for personal happiness we shall not find it. But as we go on quietly carrying out the duties and responsibilities of real life, joy will be given to us. As C. S. Lewis says, we shall be surprised at the suddenness of its coming.

> To come to the pleasure you have not
> You must go by a way in which you enjoy not.
> To come to the knowledge you have not
> You must go by a way in which you know not.

It is easy to distort John's meaning. Either we think that everything generally regarded as pleasant is to be avoided, or that the demand is only a spiritual one asking for no practical sacrifices. The truth lies somewhere in between with a balance which is different for every person. Of course pleasant things are gifts from God but certain things may be wrong for us. As Paul says in his First Letter to the Corinthians: "All things are lawful, but not all things are helpful. All things are lawful but not all things build up. . . . So whatever you do, do all to the glory of God" (10:23, 31). We see Jesus in the gospels enjoying human pleasures but always in harmony with God's honor and glory. It can be the same for us.

How, we may ask, does all this work out in practice? Let us notice, first of all, John's words "order and discretion." Exaggeration and over-zealousness are characteristics of the beginner and are likely to be followed by an equally violent reaction. All John asks is that we should *try* to give preference to those things that are contrary to our attachments. The things that we like are usually well cared for; it is the others that are pushed away and neglected. Yet we do not need to go out to seek artificial forms of unpleasantness. Our salvation lies within the realities of life, which are normally partly agreeable and partly the reverse. We need not be surprised or shocked if storms of fear, anxiety or anger sweep over us as we try in practical ways to form the habits that John recommends. If we persevere they will die down. Run away from a ghost and it will chase you; face the ghost and it will run away.

Through experience we may hope to develop a strategy for dealing with ourselves which is both tough and gentle. Bits of down-to-earth philosophy can often be more useful than wallowing in one's sinfulness before God. And there is the healing power of laughter which can suddenly break through our fraught emotions if we can stand outside of ourselves even for a moment and contemplate our own absurdity.

In any case we begin neither with negation nor morality but with love for a Person. God's love embraces everything and everyone including the difficult, the harsh, the unpleasant and the most humble, and if we want to be his disciples we must try to love as he loves. Every person has some bond to break before he or she can enter into that love. We begin by doing what we can, with the help of God, in the active night of sense.

Seeking the Father

Cf. *The Romances* I-IX

The Romances are meditations on biblical history and doctrine. They are not among the greatest of John's poems, but they do illustrate the trinitarian nature of his faith. This did not rest wholly on the personal relationship of the soul to Jesus as other poems may have led us to believe. Such a relationship can exist only because the love between the persons of the Trinity has penetrated human nature through the work of the Holy Spirit. For he is "that immense love proceeding from the Two" ("Romance II").

The first Romance may seem to be as abstract as a creed, but in those that follow we hear the voice of authentic love. The

Father speaks to the Son in words "of great affection" and we, his human children, have a place in it.

> My Son, I will give Myself
> To him who loves You,
> And I will love him
> With the same love I have for You,
> Because he has loved
> You whom I love so.

("Romance II," 7)

These poems tell the story of creation, the preparation of the world for Christ, and the incarnation, from God's point of view.

> And God would be man
> And man would be God
> And He would talk with them
> And eat and drink with them;
>
> And He Himself would be
> With them continually
> Until the consummation
> Of this world.

("Romance IV," 11 and 12)

We do not always find it easy to make the kind of relationship with the Father that Jesus knew. Sometimes we are hindered by bad early memories of earthly fathers. Images of the blood-thirsty Yahweh of the earlier books of the Old Testament may repel us. And, above all, the presence of undeserved suffering in the world may cause us to question his power or his goodness. Yet the acceptance of this area of "unknowing" proves that we are not trying to make a god in our own image. If he is the true God he will always transcend the limitations of our understanding.

Long centuries passed before the Jewish people could recognize and receive God as one who really loved them. "Romance V" speaks of the longing that gradually prepared the way for his coming. We hear the voices of the prophets:

> . . . Come Lord,
> Send Him Whom You will send!
> And others: Oh if only these heavens
> Would break, and with my own eyes
>
> I could see Him descending;
> Then I would stop my crying out.
> O clouds, rain down from your height.
> Earth needs you.

> ("Romance V," 5 and 6)

When Jesus was born the whole Trinity was involved in his incarnation. The angel was sent to Mary:

> At whose consent
> The mystery was wrought,
> In whom the Trinity
> Clothed the Word with flesh

> ("Romance VIII," 2)

Jesus tells us that those who have seen him have seen the Father. Yet throughout the ages and in the depths of our own hearts today we find the temptation to separate the Father from the Son, the judge from the accused, justice from mercy. But the Holy Spirit, who is Person as well as relationship, flows between the Father and the Son uniting and at the same time distinguishing them. In his earthly life Jesus experienced both the unity and the separation, but it was the relationship that was paramount. Jesus was the Son of God, but he was also the son of a good Jewish home and had the warm and trusting attitude of Judaism at its best. This was one of the most attractive characteristics of a rabbi friend of mine. For him Jews and Christians were equally children of the one loving Father. The children of the synagogue were encouraged to be free and spontaneous in their Father's house. In a time of great personal loss for himself he reminded us that we should not mourn for too long lest we come to think that God is not good. "We have to affirm life, not death."

How can we prepare ourselves to welcome the Trinity into our hearts? In the active night of sense we can do something, using the same methods of meditation which we used in our first approaches to Jesus. At this point we can find help elsewhere in John's writings. For instance, he includes as possible subjects for meditation not only scenes from the gospels but also God "upon a throne with resplendent majesty"; or "the imaging and considering of glory as a beautiful light" (*Ascent*, II.xii.3). As Christians, we are inclined to identify the Lover in the Song of Songs solely with Jesus. Yet in the Old Testament he represents Yahweh in his relationship with his people. Sometimes it is helpful for us to read the Song of Songs with this in mind. Then we recognize him as the initiator of love (2:4; 7:10), as the nourisher of our life (6:3), as healing ointment for our ills (1:3), as deliverer (2:10), as one with whom we can be familiar but who forever remains beyond our grasp (5:6).

Still using our senses, we can draw nearer to the Creator-God through the contemplation of nature, as John shows us in stanzas 4-7 of *The Spiritual Canticle*. In his Commentary on Stanza 4.3 he tells us that "This reflection on creatures, this observing that they are things made by the very hand of God, her Beloved, strongly awakens the soul to love Him." So John would go with his Brothers into the country as an inspiration for worship and gratitude.

But natural beauty can only partially satisfy our souls, because they are made for something more. We are led on to seek God's presence within our souls. According to John (see the Commentary to Stanza 11.3 of *The Spiritual Canticle*), he is present in three ways.

He dwells in every person, Christian or non-Christian, good and evil, whether they desire it or not. Every day the wonderful machinery of human bodies and minds is renewed. If God withdrew himself from his work of continuous creation we should instantly fall into nothingness.

Secondly, God is present by grace in the hearts of all Christians whether they are consciously aware of it or not. This grace strengthens them to keep his commandments and fight against sin.

Thirdly, God's presence may be sensed "affectively" by God's own action to make himself known. "This presence is so sublime that the soul feels an immense hidden being is there from which God communicates to her some semi-clear glimpses of His divine beauty" (*Canticle*, stanza 11.4). So in the last lines of "Romance II" the Father says,

My Son, I will give Myself
To him who loves You,
And I will love him
With the same love I have for You.

Henceforward John is addressing only those who are wholehearted in their going forward: Those who have begun to show it through the work of meditation and the active night of sense. The words, "My house being now stilled" is probably only a relative description of the state of our hearts. Yet it is enough to allow God to take over and lead us in a more direct way, which John tells us is the passive night of sense.

Interlude

Between the Nights

Cf. *The Dark Night of the Soul* I.i-vii

In these chapters John is summing up some of the characteristics commonly found in beginners who have entered into the active night of sense. He wants to show them that although they have made a good beginning they have a lot further to go. He does this by helping them "to understand the feebleness of their state" so that they may gain courage and desire for the next step.

The tone of these chapters and the examples given are colored by John's own religious culture. We need to reinterpret them according to today's spiritual and psychological insights, which are not those of the Counter-Reformation. Nevertheless the seven capital sins are with us still. A recent TV series of discussions among young people considered each of these in turn. No one denied or excused the presence of pride, avarice, lust, anger, gluttony, envy and sloth in their personal lives or in that of modern society. But John's basic assumptions were not always theirs. So in reading these chapters we should concentrate on those points that ring true to us, passing over for the time being those that do not.

John is concerned here with the left-hand "way of the imperfect spirit in goods of heaven" that we saw on the map winding its slow path round the foot of Mount Carmel. Despite all our efforts we are still at the beginning. We have not yet formed a strong habit of climbing up the center path and are easily diverted. It is true that much has happened. God has become alive for us and we have become aware of the reality of our Baptism and incorporation into Christ's dying and risen life. We are faithful to public and private prayer, work hard and honestly in our life's vocation and try to imitate Christ in our relationships and behavior. All this is good, and we cannot be expected to realize at this stage how much more there is to be done and suffered. Our spirits have been touched by God, and we expect the feelings of joy and comfort to continue indefinitely. As John says, we are spiritual babes being fed by God "with good milk and tender food."

This cannot continue for ever if we are to grow up into Christ, who knew the hardships of love in his own life. As he tells his disciples, "I have yet many things to say to you but you cannot bear them now" (Jn 16:12). The whole of the person, beginning with the senses and the emotions, needs to be brought to share in the resolute commitment made by our wills. As John describes the seven main obstacles to our progress, it can be seen that in every case a little bit of true love is mixed up with a lot of self-will and self-centeredness. There is probably some secret pride and complacency over what God has done in us, a feeling that we have won it through our own merits. Sensual pleasure may be confused with spiritual joy, and we may feel anger and resentment when it dies away. We become impatient with God and ourselves and try to recover our first rapture with exaggerated religious practices. Or we may search here and there for something that will seem to work and become over-dependent on outward aids such as books, icons or one particular person. We may be tempted to give the whole thing up in times of boredom and weariness or, alternatively, ignore advice and go off on our own. We become critical and envious of those who are considered worthier than ourselves.

We have to admit that most of this is true, but today's greater knowledge of the make-up of the human person means that pride and humility are seen in a somewhat different way. We do not think nowadays that humility involves denying our little successes, regarding ourselves as worse than everyone else, and inviting them to trample over us! The word itself is derived from *humus*, the ground and substance of reality. Humility has nothing to do with competition and everything to do with truth. How can we denigrate the wonderful work of God which is our self? It may still be immature and scarred through our own fault or that of our heredity or environment. But our security lies in God's acceptance of us as we are. He will heal and change us in his own way if we are open and willing to learn. In this respect we can identify ourselves with the humble learner of *Night*, I.ii.6-8.

John assumes that everyone will have a spiritual guide, but this may not be so today. Those who do will not have the relationship of pupil to master or culprit to judge which is implied in John's works. He lived in a patriarchal age and within a patriarchal Church. Today the emphasis is on spiritual friendship between two Christians. We feel that sin is not primarily an assortment of separate acts requiring absolution but a sickness which penetrates the whole person. The art of the soul-friend is to draw out the poison of sin so that wounds may be healed.

In *Night*, I.ii.1-6 John indicates that it is not easy for beginners to be simple and open with their guides. An atmosphere of trust and acceptance has to be created so that natural fear and pride may die away. Then there will be no need for pretence or play-acting. Nevertheless the very act of confiding, even in a close friend, invites judgement. So we have no grounds for complaint if the counsel we receive is not to our liking.

As we read John's chapters on spiritual avarice and gluttony we may acknowledge the reality of the principles while
finding some of the examples irrelevant. On the whole our
generation is not so devoted to religious bric-à-brac as our
forebears may have been. We do not weigh ourselves down
with "overdecorated images and rosaries" or "prefer one cross
to another because of its elaborateness." We do not ordinarily
deck ourselves with "relics and lists of saints' names like
children in trinkets" (*Night*, I.iii.1). However, one comment
rings very true today: "Many never have enough of hearing
counsels, or of learning spiritual maxims, or of keeping and
reading books about them" (*Night*, I.iii.1).

A vast number of methods and fashions in spirituality have
been opened up to us in recent years. Transcendental meditation, charismatic prayer, variations on Jesuit or creation spirituality, spiritual journaling, Zen Buddhist insights, work on
Myers-Briggs or the Enneagram to increase our self knowledge; all these methods, and others, may have helped us along
our spiritual path. The danger is that we may flit from one to
another, as each brings us sooner or later to the full stop which
is the beginning of the passive night of sense. We cannot
forever circle round the perimeters of prayer when God is
calling us into the still center of his nearer presence.

So each of these chapters has something to offer to modern
readers who will translate and apply John's teaching in their
own circumstances. For he says that "there are scarcely any
beginners who do not fall victim to some of these imperfections at the time of their initial fervor" (*Night*, I.ii.6). In this
respect we are no different today.

We cannot be purified only by our own efforts. "Until a soul
is placed in the passive purgation of that dark night . . . it
cannot purify itself completely from these imperfections nor
from the others. . . . God must take over and purge him in that
fire that is dark for him, as we will explain" (*Night*, I.iii.3).

3

The Passive Night of Sense

Stilling the senses

Cf.　*The Dark Night of the Soul* I.viii.3-5
　　The Ascent of Mount Carmel II.xv.1 and 2

> God now leaves them in such darkness that they do not
> know which way to turn in their discursive imaginings;
> they cannot advance a step in meditation, as they used
> to, now that the interior sensory faculties are engulfed
> in this night. He leaves them in such dryness that they
> not only fail to receive satisfaction and pleasure from
> their spiritual exercises and works, as they formerly did,
> but also find these exercises distasteful and bitter. As I
> said, when God sees that they have grown a little, He
> weans them from the sweet breast so that they might be
> strengthened, lays aside their swaddling bands and
> puts them down from His arms that they may grow
> accustomed to walking by themselves. This change is a
> surprise to them because everything seems to be func-
> tioning in reverse. (*Night,* I.viii.3)

John believes that most people who practice mental prayer
will come to know this night, often after a short time. He gives

us definite signs that show when we are ready. But he also says that some people never enter it except for short periods of time.

In the active night of sense we gain spiritual strength and enough love to bear a little darkness and dryness. The power of our attachments has been weakened and we are more ready to accept the strangeness of God's ways with us. Now we face a blankness, a full stop to the activity of our minds, whenever we try to pray. At the beginning we may need a simple image to lead us into the darkness. I remember, for example, being helped by the childish image of Alice in Wonderland following the White Rabbit down into his burrow. Soon her foot slipped, she lost control and found herself slowly falling down into the hole. Distractions were around her in the form of shelves laden with jars but she ignored them. I do not remember what happened to Alice in the end, but I found myself at the bottom in the depths of my heart where all was dark and quiet. Thoughts and images still presented themselves, but my business now was to set them aside, to remain attentive but quiet, and wait.

It is this stage which John describes as painful and bitter when it is first encountered. We find it boring and perhaps a waste of time when we could be trying to do something to help ourselves. But this is just what we must not do, as Anthony de Mello tells us.

If they avoid this evil and persevere in the exercise of prayer and expose themselves in blind faith to the emptiness, the darkness, the idleness, the nothingness they will gradually discover, at first in small flashes, later in a more permanent fashion, that there is a glow in the darkness, that the emptiness mysteriously fills their heart, that the idleness is full of God's activity, that in the nothingness their being is recreated and shaped anew . . . and all of this in a way they cannot describe either to themselves or to others. They will just know that after each such session of prayer or contemplation, call it what you will, something mysterious has been working within them bringing refreshment and nourishment and well-being with it. They will notice that they have a yearning hunger to return to this dark contemplation that seems to make no sense and yet fills them with life.

(*Sadhana* [New York: Bantam
Doubleday Dell, 1984], p.31)

In his poem "Not for all of beauty" John calls this the "I-don't-know-what of the soul." To define it more closely may sound banal. This faculty lies dormant within us, concealed below our noisy minds and the clamor of our desires. Only when God stills us can we begin to recognize its presence.

This is not an act of spiritual selfishness, a turning in when we ought to be turning out to the needs of the Church and the world. The inner darkness is in fact a well-spring of our activity and our love. It gives to our work and personal relationships a strength that we know but cannot explain even to ourselves.

John tells us that "recollected beginners" enter this night sooner than others. Fortunately, recollection does not necessarily depend on the possibility of long, quiet periods of time alone. Neither does it mean, as I used to think, that one half of our attention should be on God while the other half attends to its work. This would hardly recommend itself to employers. True recollection lies in the general direction of the self toward God. We open ourselves to him at the beginning of the day and offer ourselves for his purposes. Then he will be in our hearts, moving and controlling them even while our conscious mind is fixed wholly on what we are doing. History records the prayer of a soldier as he prepared for battle: "O Lord, you know how busy I must be this day; if I forget you, do not you forget me for Christ's sake." We do not have to approve the nature of his business to apply his sentiments to ourselves and our daily work. By faith we know that God is in the depths of our hearts, even when we do not remember him.

Although everyone needs some time to themselves if prayer is to be deepened, it can be fitted into the individual's rhythm of life and does not necessarily have to happen every day. All of us are sometimes fixed in situations in which there is nothing to do. A lot depends on how we use the minutes or hours stranded in a traffic jam on the highway, the tedious journeys on the subway or train, or the long wait in the dentist's or doctor's waiting room. Often it is when we are too tired for thought or feeling that the yearning hunger for God will draw us to the sources of life within us.

Recollection depends also on our attitude to work. The workaholic will fume and fret over every "lost" minute, but if our life is under the direction of God such moments are an essential part of life. If it is duty rather than work-addiction which keeps us busy from morning to night, that very work can be a preparation for inner prayer. Mothers with demanding families, men who are on call with emergency rescue services, people who have to work at night, anyone whose work is done willingly in a spirit of service, will find that through it their ingrained selfishness is being slowly purified. Then, when they do have time for prayer, they can often enter more quickly into it than those who have been carefully preserving their recollection beforehand.

John admits in his prologue to *The Ascent* that his Brothers and Sisters of Carmel receive a basic training in the active night of sense which most of us do not have. However, there is no short cut. According to circumstances, every committed Christian needs to take the discipline of the active night into their lives in the ways John suggests. It is dangerous to try to force an entry into our inner world without it, for we still have within us many a fear, desire and prejudice, which can emerge with devastating effect if we are not prepared.

In *Ascent*, II.xv.1 John gives guidelines for those passing from one stage of prayer to the next. If we can meditate without forcing ourselves, we may do so. Otherwise we should stop.

> The indication of this will be that every time [a person] intends to meditate, he will immediately notice this knowledge and peace as well as his own lack of power or desire to meditate. . . . Until reaching this stage . . . a person will sometimes contemplate, and sometimes meditate.

We may hope to move gradually and naturally into a deeper relationship with God, as we would do in a human friendship. Let us remember that, however clouded and confused we may feel, God continues to contemplate us and embrace us.

When to let go

Cf.   *Ascent*, II.xiii
      Night, I.ix

In these two passages John explains the signs which show that it is time to pass from meditation to contemplative prayer. They do not differ from each other in essentials, although there is variation in the detail and order in which they are given. John says that all three signs must be present if our call to go forward is a genuine one.

The first sign, as we have seen, is our inability to meditate. In *Ascent*, II. xiv John gives reasons for this. We have gained all the spiritual good that we can through using our senses in prayer. To continue would only mean a repetition of work that has already been done. Now that we have built up a habit of loving knowledge of God through our separate acts of meditation, we can enter into the place where we can experience his closer presence.

However, our Do-It-Yourself souls find this difficult at first. We mistake dryness for lukewarmness. Guilt and scruples may plague us when we feel that we are doing nothing. But if we were lukewarm we would not care. In dryness our thirst for God increases through all the boredom and darkness. "Even though in this purgative dryness the sensory part of the soul is very cast down, slack and feeble in its actions because of the little satisfaction it finds, the spirit is ready and strong" (*Night*, ix.3). John accounts for this by saying that God is transferring his goods and strength from sense to spirit.

The second sign is that, despite our lack of satisfaction in prayer, nothing else will do instead. There is no compensation outside of God. Yet this does not mean that our inner selves will be free of riotous thoughts and imaginations even when we are in deep recollection. They do not matter so long as we pay no attention to them. As we have already seen, all we can do is lay them gently aside even if we have to do it twenty times in two minutes. Gradually we distance ourselves from the turmoil, as the inner relationship with God takes control of our lives.

However, we also need the third sign, which is the ability to remain alone and still in loving awareness of God without any particular knowledge or understanding. Otherwise, our inability to meditate and our dissatisfaction with everything else may have physical or psychological causes rather than spiritual ones. It is the positive ability to be quiet in God's presence which determines whether it is right to abandon active meditation or not.

When I was first faced with these signs I found them cut and dried at one level and yet confusing at another. Perhaps I was expecting something esoteric and special. I had no idea that I was already in the state that John was describing. Yet looking back over the years I see that it was so. For he is not writing here for those who are advanced in the spiritual life but for comparative beginners. He has condensed what he has learned from the guidance of many souls into a few paragraphs. Experience confirms that what he says is true, but it may be revealed to us in a much more informal and haphazard way. The essentials of meditation may have been absorbed in the course of our Christian education. Theological and biblical study for exams; spiritual reading of the Bible, religious prose and poetry; sudden moments of understanding when scripture speaks directly to life's experience: All these may have taken us over the groundwork of formal meditation without our being aware of it. Lay Christians in John's day did not have the variety of experience which we enjoy today.

Circumstances of life may also thrust us unawares into the passive night of sense. I belong to a generation that spent long hours of boredom and short periods of terror in air-raid shelters in England during the Second World War. Family life had been abruptly shattered through evacuation and war work. Many of us no longer had a place that we could call home. Either we rode along unthinkingly on the tide of excitement and patriotism or we faced a darkness which was within as well as without. We may have been too tense and confused to meditate, but we had an aching need of God. So we were drawn, through necessity, to seek him within, finding there a point of life from which we could draw strength and peace. Once found, the prayer deepened and was further tested in the years that followed, but the initial leap had been made. In the uncertainties of life and death today, we can often do little ourselves to change the mess; but it makes all the difference to know from inner experience that God is working within it.

When John tells us in the last paragraph of *Night*, I.ix that some are called to walk the way of contemplation and some are not, he is again recording objective evidence which he cannot account for. Only God knows the reason. But this does not necessarily close the door to anyone. Most of us experience a "mid-life transition," which may include the discovery of a contemplative part of ourselves which we did not know we possessed. In any case, to be an extrovert does not prevent one from being a contemplative. In fact it may help. Outgoing people enjoy and welcome the objective reality of others. If we can transfer this capacity to our prayer we shall be less likely to see God as a projection of ourselves and more ready to receive him when he comes to us under a strange form.

However, at any given time we have to pray as we can, neither shutting the door to further possibilities nor deprecating our current mode of prayer. Yet God cannot give us an increase of spiritual gifts unless we really want it and recognize the importance and availability of these gifts in our lives.

For those who do persevere, a great, though silent, revolution will begin to take place. No longer will our identity as Christians depend on what we are doing for God. It now depends on the degree to which we can let go, allowing ourselves to become vessels for God's love and channels through which it can flow out to the world. We do not decide how and where it is to be used. We supply the waiting and the willingness.

The prayer of love and silence

Cf.   *Ascent*, II.xv
      Night, I.x

"Contemplation is nothing else than a secret and peaceful and loving inflow of God which, if not hampered, fires the soul in the spirit of love." With these words John completes the tenth chapter of *Night*, I. Here he is thinking not so much of the hampering of sin but of the obstacles which arise through our human make-up. God is like an artist trying to paint a portrait of the real self within us. If we, the incomplete model, insist on moving and fidgeting he cannot complete his work and the portrait will remain unfinished (*Night*, I.x.5).

Yet the stillness has to be of a particular quality, and there is, nevertheless, something for us to do. If we have active brains we have the work of gently discarding our thoughts as they arise. If they are more sluggish we have other problems. We may find ourselves in a grey cloud of nothingness in which the mind is quiet but vacant. This is not Christian contemplation. We need to remain attentive to the presence of a living being who is our creator, our Lord and our lover. It will more often than not be a presence by faith but none the less real for that. In this state we commune with God "more respectfully and courteously, the way one should always converse with the Most High" (*Night*, I.xii.3). So whatever our physical posture in prayer may be, whether we sit, kneel or prostrate, we remember that he is present, and that our bodies should reflect the reverence of our souls. It is possible to be happy and relaxed with a loved and honored friend without becoming what John calls "discourteous and inconsiderate."

Often we need some simple prayer to keep our attention Godward or bring it back when it has gone astray. John does not give much detailed help on this subject. However, it is summed up in one of his maxims. "Seek in reading and you will find in meditation; knock in prayer and it will be opened to you in contemplation" (*Maxims*, 79).

Our knocking is a very gentle repetition of a phrase or, better still, one word. This will be considered further in the next section. For the present let us think about the gentleness and reverence with which it should be repeated. This Christian way of prayer may seem superficially similar to non-Christian techniques, but in fact it differs in both aim and practice. Such techniques, taken perhaps from non-Christian religions, have been found useful for calming the mind, but they are not necessarily used for Christian or even religious purposes. Business firms send employees on courses of transcendental meditation because they find that a mantra can concentrate the mind, steady the emotions and release energy. Yet to repeat a word over and over again with a blank mind can act as a form of self-hypnosis or drug. This may suppress unpleasant symptoms and increase efficiency, but unless it is centered in the living God it cannot convert or heal.

So let us not bang insistently on God's door in prayer and think that he has opened it when we feel good. That is not the purpose of Christian prayer, although it may be a bonus. Sometimes we need to experience our sinfulness and poverty first.

In another maxim John says: "The Father spoke one Word which was His Son, and in this Word He always speaks in eternal silence, and in silence must it be heard by the soul" (*Maxims*, 21). So the phrase or word that we repeat should be a kind of sacrament of the Word himself. If we utter it gently in a listening spirit, the Holy Spirit within will bring to the surface what he wants to give or ask of us at any particular time. Then, in the end, our spoken words will become silence, not because we have hypnotized ourselves but because God has opened the door. "What we need most in order to make progress is to be silent before this great God with our appetites and our tongue, for the language He best hears is silent love" (*Maxims*, 53).

We may need one simple image at first in order to concentrate the mind in the heart. When speaking of this prayer John says,

> He [the worshiper] will often find that he is experiencing this loving and peaceful awareness passively without having first engaged on any active work with his faculties. But on the other hand he will frequently find it necessary to aid himself gently and moderately with meditation in order to enter this state. (*Ascent*, II.xv.2)

The image that we want to use may spring spontaneously to mind, as Alice's descent into Wonderland did to mine. If not, we might use John's own image of Jesus as the artist working in our souls. We can open ourselves to be worked upon by his loving and creative hand. Or, like Teresa of Avila, we can picture Jesus standing before us looking at us lovingly and humbly. As he looks at us lovingly, he bestows on us all that he has to give. As he looks at us humbly, he is asking for something which we alone can give. So we are joined in a circle of giving and receiving and at its heart there is silence.

The Word of God

No particular reading is suggested for this section, for nearly every page in John's works bears witness to his dependence on holy scripture. Besides his own confirmation of this in the prologue to *The Ascent*, we have the witness of those who were close to him.

> He was extremely fond of reading in the scriptures and I never once saw him read any other book than the Bible (almost all of which he knew by heart). . . . When occasionally he preached (which was seldom) or gave informal addresses as he commonly did, he never read from any book save the Bible. (From the testimony of a Brother)

So it will be appropriate for us too to take our prayer of one word or phrase from the pages of holy scripture. In the passive night of sense the Word of God is still vital, but we use it in a new way. John says that reading or meditation during our time of prayer will interfere with the work of the Spirit.

> If an individual should desire to consider and understand particular things, however spiritual they may be,

he would hinder the general, limpid and simple light of
the Spirit. He would be interfering by his cloudy
thoughts. (*Ascent*, II.xv.3)

Instead we need to immerse ourselves in Bible study at some
other time. Spiritual reading, the slow brooding over the Word
of God, will continue to build up a store of knowledge within
us which the Holy Spirit can draw upon when we come to
pray. This is not an optional extra, for without it our prayer
may degenerate into barren and meaningless repetition. Great
biblical words and phrases are rich in content and, as they are
repeated, the doors of the storehouse are opened to reveal the
treasures which we have unconsciously absorbed. We may
take the Jesus Prayer used in the New Testament by the
publican and blind Bartimeus among others. Or we may use
phrases from the Lord's Prayer. Or single words such as bread,
wine, spirit, water reveal their richness of association and
image when they are repeated.

We can say the name of Jesus also with a variety of feelings
and meanings. Adoration, thanksgiving, petition, surrender,
even honest protest and anger can color our repetition of his
name. The Holy Spirit may show him to us under a variety of
aspects as Savior, Shepherd, Teacher, Healer, Son of Man and
Son of God. If we repeat the name of God he may reveal
himself under different aspects. John tells us to "Look at that
infinite knowledge and that hidden secret. What peace, what
love, what silence is in that divine bosom. How lofty the
science God teaches there" (*Maxims*, 60).

The Holy Spirit does not act in a vacuum, and neither do
we pray alone even when there is no one else physically
present. The Word of God belongs to the whole Church on
earth and in heaven, and inspires Christian tradition. In the
biblical words which we repeat, all this is carried in us to the
Father. We shall not actively recall what our minds know, but
as we listen the Holy Spirit will bring out of our memories

things old and new. For "the Spirit helps us in our weakness; for we do not know how to pray as we ought, but the Spirit himself intercedes for us with sighs too deep for words" (Rom 8:26).

John regards this prayer as a half-way stage. Knocking with our mantra puts us into the right disposition for God to open the door in contemplation. For him that word always means a gift of God which he can give or withhold at any time. "Love is introduced as form is introduced into matter; it is done in an instant and until then there is no act but only the disposition toward it" (*The Living Flame of Love*, Commentary on Stanza 1.33).

The image has changed. Now we see chaos at the dawn of creation, bubbling and seething but impotent, for it cannot form life for itself. But God broods over the face of the waters. Suddenly his voice is heard, "Let there be light," and immediately light floods into the world. So it is with our souls. John distinguishes between those acts which emerge from our inner abyss and those with which God can suddenly enlighten us.

> Spiritual acts are produced instantaneously in the soul because God infuses them. But those the soul makes of itself . . . by means of successive desires and affections never become perfect acts of love and contemplation unless as I said, when God sometimes forms and perfects them very quickly in the spirit. (*Living Flame*, Commentary on Stanza 1.33)

These rays may come at the most unexpected times, perhaps when we least deserve them. Yet the prayer of waiting and hoping is normally the preparation for his coming. "It is vital for a person to make acts of love in this life so that in being perfected in a short time he may not be detained long, either here on earth or in the next life before seeing God" (*Living Flame*, Commentary on Stanza 1.34).

Manna in the wilderness

Cf. *Night*, I.xii and xiii

In these chapters John is describing the benefits that come to us through the passive night of sense. Because our prayer is more simple and direct, our whole life will also tend toward a greater simplicity and reality. Non-Christians may reject religion as a form of escapism, but what they are rejecting is often a travesty of the real thing. A few years ago I noticed an original Christmas display in the window of a store. Father Christmas and his reindeer had been replaced by a band of merry nuns in traditional habits gaily ringing church bells. In the eyes of those who had thought up the idea, both Father Christmas and the nuns represented a fairy-tale world far removed from the realities of everyday life. However true that may be of the world of Father Christmas, it will not be so for anyone whose Christian life is growing, even in conditions which may seem to others secluded from everyday life.

For the nearer we get to God, the more our fantasies and idealisms are challenged. We are introduced instead to the solid joys of reality. John tells us that in the passive night of sense we take off our festal garments and put on our working clothes. With the best will in the world this is no easy matter. God knows how difficult it is for human beings to come to terms with reality. So he usually enlightens us bit by bit. We come gradually to an understanding of our own incapacity, to a sober and unexaggerated realization that without God we are and can do nothing.

When this fact is accepted we find a new sense of freedom, for we recognize that our nothingness does not matter if it is held in the fullness of God. We trust him to give us everything in his good time. This was the secret of Thérèse of Lisieux, a saint of the last century who has a great appeal today for this very reason. In our heart of hearts we know that we are not supermen and superwomen, yet we demand this of ourselves and imagine that others do the same. It is true that at times we are pushed by others into roles we cannot avoid. Then it is essential that our true selves do not become identified with them. Somehow we must continue to stand before God simply and naturally as his children, not taking too much notice of the expectations and criticisms that people lay upon us.

So, as the fantasies begin to drop away, "the intellect is left limpid and free to understand the truth" (*Night*, I.xii.4). We balance the reality of our littleness with a new realization of the greatness and otherness of God. As we have seen, we are now less likely to approach him in prayer carelessly and demandingly as if he was there for our convenience. As Teresa of Avila tells us, we should not speak to the Most High as if he was our slave. And, probably without our even noticing it, temptations arising from the seven principal sins will begin to weaken their hold on us, as we are brought under the law of love. John shows us a picture of the happy state when the passive night of sense has done or is doing its work. For now, he says, greed and avarice in our spiritual life are healed, because we know that the heart of prayer does not lie in more and more spiritual experience. Impurity and spiritual lust die away when we no longer judge the quality of our prayer by our feelings. Gluttony gives place to moderation in all things. Our minds are softened by dryness and temptation so that the imperfection of our neighbors does not arouse our anger as it once did. Even if we feel envious of those who seem to be more advanced in the spiritual life than we are, this is not a spiteful jealousy. We just hope that one day we shall be like them. Likewise the sloth and boredom which we may feel in prayer have lost their undercurrent of resentment that God is so slow to show himself. Knocking in prayer can be a tedious business, but at least it shows that we are in earnest. As we discover through experience how demanding the narrow way can be, we develop a greater love and tolerance for all our fellow-Christians.

For love of neighbor is the test of the reality of our prayer in the passive night of sense. What we have been given in the darkness should be apparent in the light of day. If we really have experienced the activity of the Lord in our prayer, then we shall want to obey his commandments in our lives. And love of neighbor comes very high indeed on the list. Desire for popularity or influence or ideals of service is not enough. Only obedience to Christ's command will hold our love in the face of all the pressures that threaten to destroy it.

By this time, if they have come so far, our naïve "nuns" will be well out of their lighted shop windows and into the reality of Fifth Avenue on a cold December day. They will have learned something of the inner stillness that can be found even among the pressures of the world's business. John says that often, at this stage, God

> communicates to the soul when it least expects it, spiritual sweetness, a very pure love and a spiritual knowledge that is sometimes most delicate. Each of these communications is more valuable than all that the soul previously sought. (*Night*, I.xiii.10)

In the place that we have reached, the house of the soul is stilled from the clamor of the senses. They have been brought under the control of the spirit. Henceforward, John says, we shall know spiritual things directly through the spirit. This will be the theme of the nights of the spirit.

4

Life in the Body of Christ

Intercession

Cf. *Ascent*, III.ii.9-12

In one of the Spiritual Sayings attributed to John of the Cross it is said,

> It is clearly true that compassion for our neighbor grows the more according as the soul is more closely united with God in love: for the more we love the more we desire that this same God shall be loved and honored by all. And the more we desire this, the more we shall labor for it, both in prayer and in all necessary exercises.

John says very little about intercession as such in his works, because he would take it for granted that Christians would pray for each other as he himself did. Writing from Granada in 1587 to the nuns at Beas he says, "I commend myself to your prayers and be assured that although my charity is so little it is so directed toward you that I do not forget those to whom I owe so much in the Lord. May He be with you all."

As we have seen, something of God's own love will have been transmitted to us through the passive night of sense.

And such is the fervor and power of God's charity that those of whom He takes possession can never again be limited by their own souls or be contented with them. Rather it seems to them a small thing to go to Heaven alone. Wherefore they may strive to take many to Heaven with them. This arises from the great love which they have for their God, and it is the true fruit and effect of perfect love and contemplation. (*Spiritual Sayings* attributed to John of the Cross)

This love will be so universal that it will embrace all humanity in its suffering, sin and lovableness. "Love not one person better than another," says John, "or you will go astray." This may seem to be a near-impossible injunction, but true intercession does not discriminate and knows no bounds.

John uses the passage on intercession referred to at the beginning of this chapter to illustrate his discussion on the use of the memory in the active night of spirit. The way in which we intercede will depend on our mode of prayer at other times. No longer, therefore, will our memory be occupied in working its way through lists, sure that obligations have been fulfilled if everyone has been mentioned. Lists are helpful, but they should not become a tyranny, taking over most of the time that we have for prayer. Prayer groups that concentrate solely on intercessory prayer rarely survive. It is those which put intercession within a framework of worship and contemplation that are usually more long-lasting, for then God is at the center rather than the needs of human beings.

The prayer of attention, of gentle knocking with the one word or phrase, will therefore apply as much to intercession as it does to contemplative prayer. John says that if we wait on the Holy Spirit he will bring into our memory those for whom we should be interceding. Someone asks for our prayers, either by word or by letter. We take all that they tell us into our hearts, the place of love and caring where God himself is present. They are safe there, and we do not have to make strenuous efforts to remember facts and details. As we pray, the Holy Spirit touches our memories so that this one or that emerges and is held to God according to their need. John also believes that faces and places that we have never seen sometimes float before our inner eyes, indicating that we are meant to take them, whoever or whatever they are, into our prayers. (And if they have in fact no real existence, no harm will have been done.) In writing about intercessors, John says, "God's Spirit makes them know . . . what ought to be remembered . . . and forget what ought to be forgotten, and makes them love what they ought to love and keeps them from loving what is not in God" (*Ascent*, III.ii.9.).

We may ask what happens to those whom the Holy Spirit does not bring to our memories? Consciousness is only the tip of what we are as persons. It is the whole person who intercedes. If we have once taken somebody or something into our hearts, they are there for ever unless we consciously repudiate them. How God uses our love and our cherishing we cannot tell, but use it he does, often in ways that we shall never know.

But it may be that we shall know in the most costing and intimate way if God takes us at our word and calls us to practical action. In my case it led me, against all expectation, to Eastern Europe and Northern Ireland. If we invite in the Holy Spirit and show him our concern, we must not be surprised if our lives are turned upside down.

When we intercede it must be with respect and delicacy. God is not to be nagged and bullied into doing what we think is right. An in-between person stands on holy ground. Our work is to lay a need, a desire, a calamity simply and humbly before God, often for people who are themselves deaf and dumb in their own relationship to him. We shall not be heard for our clamor and much speaking but for the love of God and humanity which is in our hearts. It is this gift that God can use to bring good out of every evil and disaster, even among those whom we shall never meet in this life. For we are joined to God and each other by a network of threads more complex than we can ever know. Only through prayer and intercession can the human spirit travel through this labyrinth and find itself at home in all times and all places because everything is present in God.

Friends and counselors—seeking guidance

Cf. *Ascent*, II.xxii.9-13; 16-19

> Where two or three are gathered to consider what is for the greater honor and glory of my name, there I am in the midst of them—that is clarifying and confirming divine truths in their hearts (Mt 18:20). It is noteworthy that He did not say: "where there is one alone there I am"; rather He said: "where there are at least two." (*Ascent*, II.xxii.11)

This is a familiar theme in John's teaching. Although God does speak directly to our souls, that word has to be tested by the Word himself and by the Church which is his body on earth. Signs and wonders were shown to the prophets and priests of the old Covenant, because God had not yet revealed his complete revelation in Jesus. But now he has done so. "In giving us His Son, His only Word (for He possesses no other) He spoke everything to us at once in this sole Word—and He has no more to say" (*Ascent*, II.xxii.3). So every vision we may see or interior word we may hear should be judged in the light of Christ's life and teaching.

Some Christians will rely wholly on the Holy Spirit within their heart to interpret the word of Jesus to them, not through pride or self-sufficiency but because of promises which they find in holy scripture. Many others feel the need of a soul-friend but have not yet found one. John sees the giving and receiving of friendship in the Lord as an important part of the Christian way. It is an extension of the incarnation. No matter how wise we may be in advising other people, most of us have a blind spot when it comes to ourselves. We may believe passionately that some spiritual or moral proposition is true, but that passion needs to be exposed to the word of reason through someone who is not emotionally involved. So we claim Christ's promise given in Matthew 18:20 that he will be present when two or three people meet in his name. Even if we feel inarticulate and misunderstood, that promise holds good. Something will be given or asked of us through that meeting.

As a Spanish Catholic of the sixteenth century, John would have expected counsel to be provided for the most part by confessors and spiritual directors. Today, among Catholics and Protestants alike, this is not necessarily so. As we recognize that all Christians (not only professional ministers of the gospel) are representative of the Body of Christ, we become more ready to share our experience either on a one-to-one basis or in groups. This is distinct from formal confession and absolution, although the roles of counselor and confessor may frequently be combined in some Christian traditions.

We should choose our counselor with care. Just anyone will not do. For, as John says, he or she will have great influence on our spiritual life and color the direction that it takes. Who I am and the kind of person that my counselor is, do count. If we are too much alike it may be a case of the blind leading the blind. Counselors need to be rooted and grounded in their own faith and if possible have travelled some way along the interior path themselves. Unfortunately, guides with this second qualification are not easy to find. This may not matter so much if they are experienced in counselling, ready to rely on the Holy Spirit, and recognize that "God leads each one along different paths so that hardly one spirit will be found like another in even half its method of procedure" (*Living Flame*, Commentary on Stanza 3.59; see also 3.30).

John sees the relationship as one in which two persons come together to discover the truth. Then that truth is affirmed by one for the other. So we must be able to trust our friend and not impute unworthy motives or a lack of understanding if we are given advice that we do not like.

In a good relationship, mutual trust and acceptance will grow with time and patience. It does not happen by magic. It takes courage to expose ourselves, and we find every reason for not doing so. John is well acquainted with these excuses and demolishes them one by one. Strangely enough, it is sometimes harder to recognize and disclose the gifts we have received than to admit our faults. We fear that something precious will be tarnished by exposure. We are afraid of being hypocritical, proud or boastful. Nevertheless John is insistent that we should have the simplicity to share everything with our guide. "We witness humble recipients of these experiences obtain new satisfaction, strength, light and security after consulting about them with the proper person" (*Ascent*, II.xxii.16). Unless we do this they cannot guide us through the nights of the spiritual way.

John recognizes that we may need to change our counselor from time to time, for it is unlikely that one person can supply all the needs of a lifetime. "For who is there who would think that, like Paul, he could make himself all things to all men so as to win them all?" (*Living Flame*, Commentary on Stanza 3.59). So we should have that freedom, and the ex-counselor has no right to feel aggrieved! Yet we should not change our guide lightly but wait until there are clear signs that the time is right to do so.

But what of those many people who long for the help and understanding of a soul-friend and cannot find one? Most of us find ourselves in this position for at least part of our lives. Then we can turn to the saints and spiritual masters of the

Church who have shared their experience with us. It will be strange if we cannot find one whom we recognize as a kindred spirit capable of leading us to God through ways which answer our particular need. Our initial attraction may be to the spiritual poverty of Francis, the meditations of Ignatius of Loyola, the nights of John of the Cross. Yet in the end all ways open up to the fullness of Christ. The saints show us that we are never really alone. They are alive and working for us now as they did when they were on earth.

Many of us are at the same time givers and receivers of spiritual friendship. It is perhaps only when this is so that we can rightly understand the warnings and high standards that John puts before those who aspire to be spiritual guides. As we shall see, this work ought not to be taken on lightly or hastily, or we shall not only do more harm than good to others but also impede our own path to God.

Friends and counselors—giving guidance

Cf.   *The Living Flame of Love*:
      Commentary on Stanza 3.30-33; 36-38; 42-46; 53-61

When discussing the subject of spiritual guidance, the ancient fathers of the desert used to say that those who knew did not speak and those who spoke too readily did not know. When we first come to know the Lord our initial reaction may rightly be to share the good news with others. But only time can teach us the depths and range of Christian discipleship. It was refreshing to hear on the radio an interview given by a born-again Christian of twenty years' standing. When asked what those years had been like, he had to confess that in many ways they had been quite awful, what with himself, other people and the Church. Then why, the interviewer asked, had he persevered? "Because I know that God loves me and that I can be used by him," was the answer. It is just this simple witness of experience which really helps others.

John warns would-be counselors of the difficulty and delicacy of their task.

> The affairs of God must be handled with great tact and with open eyes, especially in so vital and sublime a matter as is that of these souls, where there is at stake almost an infinite gain in being right and almost an infinite loss in being wrong. (*Living Flame*, Commentary on Stanza 3.56)

Unless we are trying to accept within ourselves the pain, conflict and confusion of our own lives, we are not likely to be able to help others in their distress. Unless we are learning something of the power of the resurrection through our own death experiences, we cannot give others lasting hope. The speaker on the radio was effective because he had known both love and suffering over a long period of time.

For John it is the Holy Spirit who is the true spiritual "agent, guide and mover of souls," so that, as counselors, our chief need is for a listening ear and a caring heart rather than a too-ready tongue. For we need to discern the Spirit, who is speaking not only through us but also within the one who is being counselled. This was not a popular idea within the Catholic Church of John's day, for individual inspiration was, it was thought, an error of Protestantism. Formal meditation, on the other hand, was safe and manageable. The spiritual guide whom John compared to a blacksmith, "knowing no better than to hammer and pound with the faculties," may have been moved by the best of motives but not, in John's eyes, by the Holy Spirit.

Unfortunately it is our good intentions which can sometimes do the most harm if we are not aware of the dangers. Our human capacity for self-deception is infinite. It is only too easy for power-seeking and complacency to creep in if our clients find us helpful, and anxiety and resentment if they do not. John will have none of this. We have no right to feel jealous and angry if a soul has outgrown the help that we can give. "At least," he says, "the director should not think that he has all the requirements, or that God will not want to lead the soul further on" (*Living Flame*, Commentary on Stanza 3.57).

John has an infinite respect for the human spirit as a delicate instrument which needs to be treated as such. He compares it to a portrait painted by the Holy Spirit in subtle and gentle shades, which an insensitive counselor can damage by daubing it over with dull and harsh colors in an effort to "improve" it. "Who," he asks, "will succeed in repairing that delicate painting of the Holy Spirit once it is marred by a coarse hand?" (*Living Flame*, Commentary on Stanza 3.42).

One way in which we may tamper with the Holy Spirit's work is by trying to impose our own form of spirituality upon it. It may be that we are failing to observe and respect the way in which he is leading others, or we may be out of our depth. Then John says that we should "leave them alone and not bother with them." It is not always a good thing to share our own experiences with others, hoping to set them at their ease by showing that we understand. Often we do not. Similar experiences may have very different causes and meanings for different individuals. To interpret someone else's experience in the light of one's own may only confuse the other person and put obstructions in their path.

Today Christian and non-Christian counselors may use many of the same techniques, and both work toward health and wholeness for their clients. But for the Christian counselor this can only be found in its fullness, as the life of Christ is made manifest in the soul. So John tells spiritual guides that their work is to help others toward that freedom which God intended for the human race from the beginning. "Pacify the soul, draw it out and liberate it from the yoke and slavery of its own weak operation . . . which is the captivity of Egypt. . . . And guide it to the land of promise flowing with milk and honey" (*Living Flame*, Commentary on Stanza 3.38). The ultimate aim of the counselor is to be no longer needed, so that on the other side of the nights of sense and spirit the soul will be able to "stand upright on his own feet with his spirit completely detached from everything" (*Living Flame*, Commentary on Stanza 3.36).

Community

Cf. *Counsels to a Religious*

All of us spend at least part of our lives in close association with others, whether our community is a family, a school, a work-place, a church group or a religious order. One thing that all these groupings have in common is human nature. It is likely to be the cause of most of our troubles as we try to tread the Christian way. Therefore, although I am tempted to pass over John's comments on community living, it would not be fair to him or to the reader to do so.

The minor works of John which have survived were collected together from community conferences, letters and the memories of individuals, and were addressed mainly to the friars and nuns of his own Order. So they are heavily colored with the ideals of a particular age and a special vocation. We have to search diligently to find what can help us today in the *Counsels to a Religious*, the *Precautions*, the *Letters* and the various collections of *Maxims* and *Sayings* which have been passed down to us. The *Counsels to a Religious* were written for a beginner, a lay brother, perhaps, or a student.

The attitudes and principles which are recommended are not likely to pass unchallenged by the modern reader. Much depends on our approach. We may stand on our own ground looking across a gulf of four hundred years to the strange world on the other side, and judge it by our own standards. We remain outside so that it cannot contribute anything of its inner life to us. Or we can follow John's maxim, *"Where there is no love, put love in and you will draw out love."* Psychological attitudes and moral values shift and change with time; love is the only eternal imperative. With love and imagination we can enter into John's world and draw out from it what is applicable to us today.

In the first Counsel, for example, John preaches resignation to things as they are, and the avoidance of questioning, criticism or interference. "You should live in the monastery as though no one else were in it." Today we would see little point in belonging to a community in which we had no part in the decision-making. We may reflect that it was the Good Samaritan who did interfere, rather than the priest and Levite who did not, who received commendation from the Lord. As children of the Creator-God we are obliged to add our active contribution to the common mind and the common good. Otherwise we are failing in obedience to his intentions for us.

But if we enter with deeper sympathy into what John is saying, our viewpoint may be modified by his. We have to admit that today, as then, anxiety, interference, curiosity and gossip blur our inner relationship to God and to others as nothing else can. When we love, we trust; when we trust, we are ready to leave people alone to get on with their lives and their work until they indicate their need and desire for help. As love grows, we come to recognize whether our instinct to intervene indeed comes from God or from our own busy ego.

The second Counsel reminds us that we are living stones that form a community, forever being shaped and chiselled by the thoughts, words and deeds of others.

Some will chisel with words, telling you what you would rather not hear; others by deed, doing against

you what you would rather not endure; others by their
temperament, being in their person and in their actions
a bother and annoyance to you; and others by their
thoughts neither esteeming nor feeling love for you.
(*Counsels*, 3)

Far from being an obstacle, John sees this fact of life as an
opportunity for growth in love. But if it is to be used fruitfully
today, our motivation, self-image and understanding of conflict may differ from his. If we endure patiently merely to gain
virtue for ourselves, are we not claiming the role of victim and
thereby imposing that of aggressor on everyone else? It is the
fact that we are all sometimes aggressors and sometimes
victims that binds us together in a mutuality which can itself
be a source of unity. Our creative work is to bring greater love
and life out of this conflict for the benefit of all. We cannot do
this if we are forever turning in on ourselves in defensiveness
and self-loathing. It is acceptance of ourselves in our imperfection which sets us free to love others in theirs.

Yet the purpose of any community and family transcends
the personal desires of its members for security, peace and
understanding. If these things come, it is as a bonus rather than
a right.

Conflict is part of the common struggle of a group to achieve
its aims and purposes, and our ideas on how this should be
done usually differ. Those who chisel us often have no idea of
the hurt that they cause, any more than we know what we do
to them. We shall make heavy weather over everything and
everyone if we see them through a cloud of our own imagin-
ings. For then, John says, "You will not know how to overcome
your sensitiveness and feelings, nor will you get along well in
the community . . . nor attain holy peace, nor free yourself
from many stumbling blocks and evils" (*Precautions*, 15).

In the third Counsel, John tells us that everything we do
should be done for God's glory, whether it be weighty or

humble, congenial or unpleasant. Nevertheless he recommends the most humble and onerous choices as the most virtuous. Today we may question whether we should acquire this virtue at the expense of others. We may ask what kind of a God it is that equates virtue with the difficulty or unpleasantness of the task. In fact, it is our own moral guilt that projects these judgements on to him. If our basic desire is for God's glory we shall not have to worry about our place in the hierarchy of virtue. Everything that contributes to the common purpose is good and honest. We could hardly recommend someone with a heavy mortgage to choose the lowest place at work, nor evade responsibility for ourselves if it comes our way. But in everyday life and in any community the difficult members, the necessary but boring chores, are always with us. Jesus awaits us there if we approach him and them with love, not with self-conscious virtue.

The fourth Counsel concerns solitude and inner recollection and is addressed to a beginner. Unless we remember this, we may feel, in the words of one reader, that John "is horribly stand-offish and playing for safety the whole time." It needs a conscious effort to transfer our motivation from self-centered to God-centered ends. This may involve a greater or lesser degree of physical withdrawal in order to establish and reaffirm our unique relationship with God. In this solitude we can more readily discover who we are and what our place is to be in the whole. But we all need an inner solitude which will not appear stand-offish to others unless they are requiring a greater degree of emotional involvement than we can give. In a family, and even more in a larger community, love has to be spread over a number of people and our narrow human hearts cannot cope. Only God's love flowing through us will instinctively sound the right chord. Our love will not be depersonalized, but the content of anxiety will be removed from it as we realize that others belong to his love before they belong to ours.

For a Christian the increase of love through community is the purpose which embraces and transcends all other specific aims. If it does not do so, love fades into observance of the law, morality takes its place, and community life hardens into rigid shapes and forms.

We must not be too fundamentalist in our reading of the *Counsels*. The way in which they are worked out will vary with our circumstances, which certainly will not be those of John. But if we are open to the Spirit rather than dismissive, we shall find an inner wisdom which is as applicable to the twenty-first century as it was to the sixteenth. We are all children of the one unchanging Father.

Interlude

The Way Ahead

Cf. *Ascent*, II.i.1; iv

In our journey of faith we have come to an important point. At the beginning of *The Ascent*, as we have seen, John explained that there were three reasons for calling the journey toward God a night. The first involved the deprivation of sensual support, which is a characteristic of both earthly and spiritual nights. Through self-discipline and God's direct action we began to be free of undue attachments to material things. We practiced using our senses for his glory. We did not do this without pain and darkness, for we were treading a hitherto unknown path. Yet, even so, there was a little light on the way. We could see something of what God had already done in us and definite ways in which our lives had been changed.

Now we are being invited to open ourselves to a more complete darkness, which is the way of pure faith. God wants to penetrate more deeply to the well-springs of our actions, which lie in our intellects, memories and wills. These faculties make up what John calls the "rational superior part" of the soul. Until they are purified by faith, hope and charity they do not know how to operate as God intends. They are at the mercy of our self-centeredness and human limitations. Our thoughts and feelings are colored by ourselves and our interests, our relations and our friends, our work, our nationalism, our religion and politics. It is inevitable that this should be so. But if we mistake for ultimate reality the small part of truth which we have been given, we are hampering the development of Christ's life within us.

Inner change begins with prayer, although it does not end there. John says,

> A man, then, is decidedly hindered from the attainment of this high state of union with God when he is attached to any understanding, feeling, imagining, opinion, desire or way of his own, or to any other of his works or affairs, and knows not how to detach or denude himself of these impediments. His goal transcends all of this, even the loftiest object that can be known or experienced. (*Ascent*, II.iv.4)

The door of faith opens up into an unknown country into which God will draw us if we are willing to let go of the security of clinging to what we know.

But the life of Christ does not keep prayer in one compartment and the practical business of living in another. In *Ascent*, III.xviii-xlv (which we shall be considering in detail later), John shows how sense and spirit can work together in all areas of life in a hierarchy of love. If joy in God transcends yet includes all our lesser joys, then they find their true meaning in him. We establish our priorities in the active night of spirit and spend the rest of our lives trying to keep them in their right order and proportion.

We learn in the public and private areas of our life that it is our inner orientation which makes all the difference to the way in which our life is lived. An example from Northern Ireland may serve to illustrate this. Here a predominantly Catholic and nationalist culture lives side by side with one that is mainly Protestant and British. Both groups have more in common than they realize, but it is often the prejudices, fears and fantasies rather than the reality which control the lives of individuals. I remember an outburst from a young Protestant man whom I encountered on the walls of Derry. He had been shocked by the devastation done to one of the historically holy places of Protestantism by IRA bombs and British Army barbed wire. His feelings were too much for him. Looking out over the ramparts to Catholic Bogside, he spat out his anger and contempt with three hundred years of bitterness in his voice. It would be only too easy for an English Anglican to dismiss this violence with repugnance and superiority. Yet below it lay a mourning for something precious, a way of life that had nurtured himself and his ancestors and was being destroyed. Likewise, in greater or less measure, we all react with anger when we feel that our lesser gods of family, race or creed are under threat.

We love and cling to these gods because there is so much that is good about them. But God's commandment, "You shall have no other gods but me," challenges our creeds, history and limited experience. It may seem to demand a rejection of all that we hold sacred and dear. This is not so. In the active night of spirit we learn that we do not have to feel guilty about our lesser loves nor seek to dismiss them from our lives. However, our relationships need to bear upon them the mark of our deeper love for God. And that is the mark of the cross.

It is painful and difficult for most of us to use our imaginations rightly and to go against deep-rooted customs and conventions if God seems to demand it. Almost impossible, we may think, when looked at in human terms. Yet John points forward into the realms of faith, where the impossible becomes possible in ways that we cannot know beforehand. Until the end of 1989, the Communist empire in Eastern Europe appeared to be fixed and immovable. Yet within a year it was broken open. It is true that revolution brought with it chaos and instability, yet it carried within itself the seeds of hope. In such a situation there is room for the Holy Spirit to work.

So it can be with us if we have the courage to let go of our lesser props and stays. For the cross is never an end in itself but a passage to new life on the other side.

5

The Active Night of Spirit

The journey of the cross

Cf. *Ascent*, II.vii

> By it [His death, Christ] . . . accomplished the most
> marvelous work of His whole life, surpassing all the
> words and deeds and miracles that He had ever per-
> formed on earth or in heaven. That is, He brought about
> the reconciliation and union of the human race with
> God through grace. (*Ascent*, II.vii.11)

> A man makes progress only through the imitation of
> Christ, who is the Way, the Truth and the Life. (*Ascent*,
> II.vii.8)

The whole of creation, and humanity as its priest, is marked
with the sign of the cross. We may avoid it, build up defenses
against it, or try to use it positively as John recommends. What
we cannot do is assume that it will go away with enough social
engineering. It will not, for it is an essential element in our
growth as human beings and followers of Christ.

Let us notice first of all that suffering is not meant to drive
us permanently into ourselves. Admittedly, when it is bad
enough we can think of nothing else. Nevertheless it points

toward something beyond ourselves. John sees Christ's cross as a work "surpassing all the words and deeds and miracles that He had ever performed." As members of Christ, the sufferings that we encounter in life can be the means of carrying on his work in the world today. This is not a popular fact and never was.

> Few there are with the knowledge and desire for entering upon this supreme nakedness and emptiness of spirit. As this path on the high mount of perfection is narrow and steep, it demands travellers who are not weighed down by the lower part of their nature, nor burdened in the higher part. (*Ascent*, II.vii.3)

We can only know resurrection life through the cross. It is a life of faith because the other side of suffering is always something that we could not have foreseen.

The cross goes deeper than the inconveniences we experience in following the customs of a religious culture. Many spiritual people, says John, make the mistake of thinking that this is enough. "Some are content with a certain degree of virtue, perseverance in prayer and mortification, but never achieve the nakedness, poverty, selflessness or spiritual purity . . . that the Lord counsels" (*Ascent*, II.vii.5).

Such people serve the Lord only for the comfort and consolation they receive. The nakedness and emptiness are summed up in the difficult word "annihilation." My dictionary defines this word as "reduction to nothing; the destruction of soul as well as body." For instance, John tells us that Christ was annihilated in his reputation, his human death and his apparent abandonment by the Father. Yet his essential being remained, to be resurrected by that same Father. In our nights we may feel annihilated, but that is not the same thing as being so. The destruction of soul as well as body applies to hell rather than to the life-giving death of the cross.

Our individual crosses are as unique to ourselves as our fingerprints. They come through our bodies, our personalities, our heredity and our environments. They are the raw material of our spiritual growth. It is easy to be thankful for much that God has given us. About the rest we are none too sure. Sometimes it is the smallest things that cause the most agony. This is why we can never bear others' sufferings for them, no matter how much we want to be identified with them in it. We can never know the exact point of pain, nor the inner strengths that God has provided for them alone. Of course we sometimes need professional help in understanding and treating our minds and bodies. Yet it is the spirit within which determines whether we suffer healthily or destructively. This is especially difficult to understand when the sickness appears to be of the mind, such as schizophrenia and some forms of depression. It may be that the disease is never healed medically and yet the sufferer finds acceptance, faith and even humor within the situation. We recognize and respect the spiritual maturity of such people and the families that support them. We cannot be complacent about the suffering of others; we need to do all we can to relieve it. Yet in the lives of individuals we see God writing straight with crooked lines, and we can only marvel at the mystery of the cross.

The faith, hope and love toward which John points us in the active night of spirit enable us to bear our crosses healthily and positively. There are times, especially in sickness, when it is impossible to pray consciously. Yet at the depths of our being we can be helped by virtues which were built up when we were well. Our understanding is helped by faith, as we cling to the promises found in God's Word. Our memory is fed by hope that trusts in the goodness of our heavenly Father: Such hope is based on recollection of the good rather than the bad things that have happened to us in the past. Our will is helped by charity, in which we respond in obedience to what we think he is asking of us even though we do not know its meaning.

By this means we find Christ's yoke to be easy and his burden light. "If a man resolutely submits to the carrying of this cross, if he decidedly wants to find and endure trial in all things for God, he will discover in all of them great relief and sweetness" (*Ascent*, II.vii.7).

So John emphasizes, "The journey, then, does not consist in recreations, experiences and spiritual feelings, but in the living, sensory and spiritual, exterior and interior death of the cross" (*Ascent*, II.vii.11).

Faith and understanding

Cf. *Ascent*, II.v.6-11; viii.4-7; xiv.8-10

In Books II and III of *The Ascent* John describes the influence of the active night of spirit on the functioning of our minds, memories and wills. As Christians, most of us are probably involved from time to time in theological discussions with non-believers and are often conscious of a hidden element in the exchange. We feel that we are communicating on two different levels. The honest non-believer thinks that logical argument is the only respectable way of discovering truth and does not understand how limited this is in the affairs of the spirit. Christians know that they must give a good account of themselves on the intellectual level and yet are well aware that ultimate truth lies elsewhere. It is the element of faith that makes the difference.

Many non-believers have high moral principles stemming from their own philosophies of life. But a Christian's moral goodness does not depend on a principle but on a Person. God's life flows continually into ours, gradually transforming our human faculties so that they come to act with his life rather their own. In the active night of spirit we try to work alongside God, laying aside our old ways of using our inner powers when we find that they are contrary to his. Therefore John says that all spiritual growth depends on the cleansing of our faculties. He compares the soul to a smudgy window through which a pure ray of light is trying to pass. The cleaner the window, the more light can get through. If it was completely clean it would become one with the sun's rays and shine like it (*Ascent*, II.v.6).

The smudges are caused not only by sin but by our psychological reactions to God's coming, which we may confuse with the true light. When we sense his presence it may be through a cloud of thoughts, feelings, images and judgements. While this is usually inevitable, they are only side-effects of what is actually happening in the depths of our being. The preparation for union does not lie in any of these things but in the "purity and love which is the stripping off and perfect renunciation of all these experiences for God alone" (*Ascent*, II.v.8).

Yet in another image we see that God does use our natural faculties as a means toward the end. John now pictures the entry of God into our souls as a single ray of sunlight piercing through a dusty room. We can see it only because the specks of dust in the air reflect the light and give it substance (*Ascent*, II.xiv.9 and 10). If there was no dust we would experience light as darkness, as cosmonauts have found when they passed out of the earth's atmosphere. So to pure faith the light of God in the soul appears as darkness. What we see are the remaining specks of dust which show up clearly in the light and enable us to welcome a God whom we could not otherwise recognize.

From chapter x to the end of the second book of *The Ascent*, John lists in detail the ways in which God uses natural and supernatural modes of perception, with a view to helping the individual soul penetrate the divine darkness. The terms that he uses are technical and may present difficulties for a modern reader unfamiliar with the language of scholastic theology. So the following brief synopsis may be useful in showing John's purpose to be sorting out the spiritual from the psychological elements in the various kinds of communications he mentions. These psychological factors may fluctuate with age and condition, but the essential spiritual core of our relationship with God is of eternity, for it is founded on faith.

John begins by telling us that not every type of inner communication necessarily comes from God; it may have its origin in ourselves or in the devil. Whatever its source, the communication will be seen or heard through the senses or received interiorly through the intellect or the imagination. For instance, we may actually see visions similar to those of Lourdes or, more recently, Medjugorje. More likely, we shall form pictures in our imagination or they may appear before our eyes of their own accord. Throughout the Christian centuries people have come to God through such means. John accepts these visions as a beginning or an encouragement to faith, but not as the substance of it. Since he considers that people think too much of such things, he uses a large part of *Ascent* II to put them into proportion.

Next, John describes spiritual communications that come through the intellect rather than the imagination. We are suddenly shown a deep and penetrating truth about God's being, or the world and human life, or a doctrine of the Church which until now has been a mere form of words. John feels happier with these as they "are already interior, purely spiritual and less exposed to the devil's meddlesomeness" (*Ascent* II.xxiii.4). Nevertheless caution is still needed and consultation with one's spiritual adviser.

The same is true of "locutions," words that we may hear within us which we believe come from God. John speaks of "successive locutions," which the Holy Spirit may give us in the course of prayer; "formal locutions," which we may suddenly hear when we are thinking of something quite different; and "substantial locutions." These are words which immediately bring into effect what they say. For instance, in a time of danger or stress we may suddenly hear the words of Christ,

"Peace I leave with you, my peace I give to you," and immediately feel his peace within our hearts.

John says that our attitude to all these gifts should be the same. We thank God for them and put them into our store of faith without any further thought. If we rely on them too much they will ultimately cramp our spiritual growth. For although we think the outward signs to be great, God is, at the same time and unknown to ourselves, pouring far more of his Spirit into the hidden depths of our souls.

This hiddenness may confuse and offend the unbeliever, and as Christians we do not find it easy either. We long to see and feel something concrete in our prayer, some assurance that a personal God is there. Only as we come to accept the inevitability of darkness do we discover its reliability. God does guide us and answer our prayers, but normally he does not tell us beforehand what he is going to do. What is being tested, then, is not his faithfulness but our faith. In the night we grow up to become the children of God, for we go beyond what "blood, or the will of the flesh, or the will of man" can compass. We put our intelligence under the Holy Spirit's guidance, at least in intention. Only practice will make this aspiration a reality.

Memory and hope

Cf. *Ascent*, III.ii.8-12; xv.1

In the first verse of *Ascent*, III.xv John summarizes his teaching on the union of the memory with God through hope. Hope, in the sense in which he uses the word, is not to be confused with vague optimism. It is solid trust in a Person on whom we can rely, whose love and power can redeem even this wayward faculty.

In this life we cannot tell how much or how little of our

memory has been given into God's hands, for so much is hidden in the unconscious. When we try to spread it out before us we find patchiness even in those areas which are available to us. In one aspect our memory is a treasure house full of beautiful objects, but in another it is a dustbin of remnants of which we are ashamed. Below all this is the vast unknown world of corporate memories inherited from our families, our culture and our race. These strata are below our complete understanding and will-power, and we have no alternative but to trust in God who is familiar with the whole labyrinth. John says that the more our primal hope remains free of lesser props and stays, the more it will hold us to God. "This is our task now with our memory. We must draw it away from its natural props and capacities and raise it above itself . . . to supreme hope in the incomprehensible God" (*Ascent*, III.ii.3).

When phrased in modern language, John's practical advice is simple to comprehend although less simple to practice. Whenever an "idea, form or image" presents itself either from our own mind or from that of someone else, we should stand back from it before responding. Otherwise our immediate response to current situations may be dominated by conscious and unconscious memories which distort the impartiality of our response. When we do react with exaggerated joy, fear, or anger we often do not know why. These reactions imprison us in a false, superficial self from which it is difficult to extract ourselves. Then other people feel that they cannot trust our moral judgement. So when we are suddenly faced with demands or injustices which seem too much to bear, we need to take time, a few minutes, a few hours, sometimes even a few days or months, to hold the situation and our emotions to God. He is the factor that can break the dreary chain of cause and effect, which may stretch back into infancy or even the womb.

So we can hope to reach a point at which what had previously seemed impossible now opens up a way before us. We find ourselves taking the next step with calmness and composure, because we are now responding in the present moment. Now the Holy Spirit can guide us. As John says, "At a particular time a person will have to attend to a necessary business matter. He will not remember through any form, but without his knowing how, the time and suitable way of attending to it will be impressed on his soul without fail" (*Ascent*, III.ii.11).

This does not overrule or interfere with the natural processes of learning and remembering. If we thought that we could rely on God without doing the necessary work for an examination, that would be reliance on magic rather than trust. However, there is a time for amassing information and a time for letting it go into the hands of God to allow him to illuminate, draw out and bind together what we already know in the depths of our memory. When we learned to swim we went through all the necessary movements by the side of the swimming pool. But once we had learned to trust ourselves to the water we thought very little about what our arms and legs were doing. John goes so far as to say that the works of the memory become in some way divine if they are controlled by the Holy Spirit.

In the course of moving from the natural to the supernatural use of our memory there may be an awkward phase in which a person "will forget to eat or drink or fail to remember whether or not he performed some task, or saw a particular object, or said something" (*Ascent*, III.ii.8). Yet once people have the habit of relying on the guidance of the Holy Spirit, they do not experience these lapses but in fact manage practical affairs better than before.

Everything that John advises at this stage can apply equally to prayer. The treasure house of our memory may contain many precious things which we think essential to our spiritual well-being. Many of these may center around aids to prayer and particular places and people. John includes among them the use of rosaries, images, special places of pilgrimage, special forms of prayer. In a Reformed tradition our devotion may center around a particular church or chapel, a preacher, a version of the Bible. These aids are not to be despised or rejected but treated "with an honor that is relative" (as the Orthodox say of icons).

John's teaching about not clinging to memories in *Ascent*, III.iii-xiv is similar to that which he has given on faith and the intellect. We should only hold on to past spiritual experiences if they lead us to a renewed love for God. For in prayer as in living we do not forget our Creator. The memory of him feeds our hope as we use the past to lead us safely through the present into the future that he has in mind for us.

Silence and distraction

Cf. *Ascent*, III.iii; v; vi

Many who read this book will have been in retreat from time to time. We go to some quiet and beautiful place where conditions for prayer should be ideal. When we first arrive we feel our cares and responsibilities dropping away, as we sink into the silence and peace. It will not be the fault of our surroundings if we cannot pray. So it is all the more disconcerting if we wake next morning to a barrage of inner noise and clamor which we hardly knew we had within us. In fact it was there all the time concealed by activity and the demands of other people. Now it is making itself known.

We are afraid that all our precious time is going to be wasted, for we may not know the right way to deal with the clamor within us. Our first instinct will probably be to fight against it, feeling that with a little more will-power it will be driven away. John says that this is not so.

> You may say that a man is easily capable of conquering all these dangers when they come on him. I reply that it is simply impossible to achieve this completely if one

pays attention to this knowledge, for intermingled with it are a thousand imperfections and trifles. . . . These imperfections are better overcome all at once through the complete denial of the memory. (*Ascent*, III.iii.4)

In the previous section we thought how this could be done with particular memories and desires. Now John advises similar treatment for the mass of undifferentiated thoughts within us. If we poke around in the garbage heap all we shall find is garbage.

In giving this counsel, he points out in *Ascent*, III.ii.1 that he is not writing for beginners but for those who are in the way of the active night of spirit. Beginners may need to use their senses and memory a great deal to bring to the surface the story of their lives. Trauma and shock can bring a forgetting but not in the sense that John means. Wounds, sometimes very deep-seated, need to be felt again with the emotions of anger and depression or pain which they caused in the first place. A friend or counselor may help us along the path of acceptance and healing of the memories. Even so, it is likely that we shall carry some wounds and scars for the rest of our lives. Yet in the end we may find peace in those experiences which unite us to Christ and his cross and to our fellow men and women whom we often cannot help in any other way.

Then we can simply put all the jumble of our memories into the hands of the Holy Spirit without psychological explanations or excuses. "It is better to learn to silence and quiet the faculties so that God may speak. For in this state . . . the natural operations must fade from sight. This is realized when the soul arrives at solitude in these faculties and God speaks to its heart" (*Ascent*, III.iii.4).

This will not happen all at once and maybe not for many years. We shall need to return time and time again to our inner center when our thoughts and daydreams escape from our control. We cannot measure our progress in terms of freedom from temptation but only by the speed or otherwise with which we return home after any falling away. We pay no attention to the wayward thoughts, which dance around in our minds like a thousand little devils, ignoring them even when they disguise themselves as angels of light. Gradually, if given no encouragement, they will go away. Then we may be aware of a small pool of silence and strength within us, which is the core of genuine peace.

Among these thoughts will be worry, the most seductive yet the most profitless of them all. Sometimes we equate worry over other people with prayer for them, which it certainly is not. We are in fact failing to hope in God and in the people themselves. For he will have given them their own secret resources and strengths to which we have no admittance. Our part is to hold them in his love unless and until there is a strong indication that something practical is asked of us. "For the afflictions and disturbances engendered in a soul through adversities are no help in remedying these adversities; rather, distress and worry ordinarily makes things worse and even does harm to the soul itself" (*Ascent*, III.vi.3).

John, in common with his contemporaries, believed in a personal devil who is always ready to inflame our memories. He does not, however, speak of devil-possession, which is very rare in fact if not in fantasy. Nowadays we may have different ideas about the power of evil. We may believe that the devil is a self-created projection of all that we dislike about ourselves. Or we may believe that there is a spirit of evil in conflict with the spirit of God throughout the universe. Even holy ideas and forms are open to attack. In any case he or it does not have to work very hard to stir up our inner fear, guilt, pride and shame. So John advises silence, emptiness and nakedness so that this power has nothing to work upon.

The soul should remain closed then, without cares or afflictions, for He who entered the room of His disciples bodily while the doors were closed . . . and gave them peace, will enter the soul spiritually (without its knowing how or using any effort of its own) once it has closed the doors of its intellect, memory and will to all apprehensions. And He will fill them with peace, descending upon them as the prophet says, like a river of peace. (*Ascent*, III.iii.6)

The pattern of Christ's life and suffering is laid upon every baptized Christian whether it is recognized or unknown, accepted or avoided. But Christian hope confidently awaits its resurrection even in this life. Our Easter may dawn slowly and gradually with no sudden blaze of light, but we shall come to know it for what it is, the pledge of our future transformation.

Charity and the will

Cf. *Ascent*, III.xvi and xvii

The First Letter to the Corinthians tells us that faith and hope are nothing without charity, and John repeats the same truth as he completes his teaching on the human faculties. Charity turns away from all that is contrary to God, preserving all its strength for him, "and comes to love Him with all its might."

In choosing a biblical text to illustrate this, John says:

I have found no more appropriate passage than the one in Deuteronomy where Moses commands, "You shall love the Lord your God with all your heart and with all your soul and with all your strength" (Dt 6:5). This passage contains all that a spiritual man must do and all that I must teach him here if he is to reach God by union of the will through charity. (*Ascent*, III.xvi.1)

For John the word charity means a love which is first of all directed toward God. We love and serve our fellow human beings because God desires it. "Through charity, works done in faith are living works and have high value; without it they are worth nothing" (*Ascent*, III.xvi.1). Mother Teresa of Calcutta is an example of someone with such priorities. No one could confuse her service of the outcast and dying with that of secular humanism or do-goodery. As she herself says, "We are not social workers; we are first and foremost contemplatives."

Our attitudes toward life, ourselves and other people depend more than we may realize on our relationship to God. If we look on him solely as a supplier of good things we have not gone deeply enough into the mystery of suffering. If we regard him as an all-powerful king we may be too passive, unlike the Old Testament Jews who questioned him confidently and often. If our Christian faith is exclusively cross-centered we may never let ourselves believe in a life of resurrection. John knew it even in the darkness of his prison. Maybe we cannot go that far, but if there is even a grain of charity in our suffering we may look back on it afterward as a time of rebirth.

John tells us that God has given human beings the stewardship of their own wills. He gives us faculties, passions and appetites that we need to learn to control and use like a team of horses. But it is charity, inspired by God, which leads us to drive our team in his direction and under his guidance rather than along the many side roads that attract and seduce us.

We are led astray by what John calls "inordinate feelings," which drain off our strength through our appetites, loves and works and sometimes leave very little room for God. He describes the four main feelings and passions as joy, hope, sorrow and fear, which are neither good nor bad in themselves. What matters is the use we make of them. When they are directed toward God "the individual rejoices only in what is purely for God's honor and glory, hopes for nothing else, feels sorrow only about matters pertaining to this and fears only God" (*Ascent*, III.xvi.2).

The more the feelings and passions are turned to other things the more the soul becomes dependent on created beings and the less it feels for God. It then very easily "finds joy in what deserves no rejoicing, and hope in what brings it no profit, and sorrow over what should perhaps cause rejoicing and fear where there is no reason for fear" (*Ascent*, III.xvi.4).

In the next twenty-nine chapters of Book III, John describes the different ways in which our love for God can be diluted by the joy of the will in lesser things. We may rejoice because we are comfortably off and have a respected position in the community. Or our natural gifts and beauty may be a source of satisfaction to us. We may rest in things that please the senses such as beautiful scenery, music or good food. Or we may feel complacent because we are morally righteous and psychologically well-balanced, or because we have exceptional supernatural and spiritual gifts. We may even dwell with satisfaction on the amount of spiritual growth which we have achieved.

Many of these things may lead us to God if they are accepted and used as gifts rather than personal possessions. Nowadays we know that spiritual and earthly goods cannot be put into separate compartments. The human person is one whole. Yet even though we affirm that all created things are contained in God we still have attitudes which determine whether they are good or bad for us. It is these which concern John.

We have the potential to enjoy the freedom of the children of God—and often do not want it because we do not know what it is. Liberation Theology invented a clumsy but expressive word, "conscientization." The peasants of South America had no idea that they had social and political rights until someone told them so. Similarly, before the advent of the feminist movement women did not understand the degree to which they were handicapped in most walks of life. Now at any rate they recognize the possibilities that could be open to them. So it is in our spiritual lives. John tells us that we have the possibility of an inner freedom that goes beyond anything that we have known. He shows us the active steps that we can take in order to claim it.

In the following chapters of *Ascent*, III, he describes six of the chief ways in which sense and spirit working together can lead us either to joy and freedom in God or limit us in a slavery which is no better for being cherished. We may feel that we have met all this before in the active night of sense. However, the will is now being involved at a far deeper level, as God purifies and renews spirit and soul together.

As we see in *Ascent*, III.xvi.3 John meant to describe one by one the effects of hope, fear and grief upon the soul. Unfortunately this book breaks off abruptly so that even the discussion on joy is curtailed. However, as "these four passions are so brother-like that where one goes actually the others go virtually," we can believe that we have received the substance of his teaching.

6

Sense and Spirit

Joy in temporal goods

Cf. *Ascent* III. xviii and xx

> By temporal goods we mean: riches, status, positions
> and other dignities, and children, relatives and mar-
> riages, etc. All these are possible objects of joy for the
> will. (*Ascent*, III.xviii.1)

John says that we should rejoice in temporal goods only if we
serve God through them. This is the teaching of the Old and
New Testaments. He quotes passage after passage to show
that love of God and love of riches cannot exist together in the
human heart. However, as we read these chapters we realize
that John is talking about two kinds of joy in material goods,
the possessive and non-possessive. In chapter xviii he appears
to grudge even our joy in marriage and children. Yet when we
turn to chapter xx.2 we find that it is not the things themselves
that are impure but rather the selfish and self-seeking attitudes
toward them which we confuse with real love.

In chapter xix John describes four stages through which joy
in God will decrease if dependence on material things grows.
In the first, our attachments may only be trifling but neverthe-

less they tend to darken our judgements and weaken our wills. If we do not realize that harm has been done we are very likely to stretch out our hands for more. Inevitably we begin to lose interest in the things of God. "The trait of those in this second degree is extreme lukewarmness in spiritual matters and carelessness about them" (*Ascent*, III.xix.6). In the third degree God is abandoned and our whole will becomes centered on what we can acquire in this world. The fourth stage is that of the miser in whom possessions have taken the place of God.

However, as we read these chapters on joy in temporal goods we should notice that John does not once use the word poverty. He never regarded material want as anything but an evil, which he would relieve whenever he could. We read of the alms that he begged for a poor priest to buy a new cassock and for a nun to purchase a pair of shoes. He himself had known extreme poverty in his youth and knew that when it is real, people cannot think of anything beyond their next meal. So they are tied down by their need as securely as rich people may be by their possessions. In either case they are hindered from attaining their destiny as children of God.

Our way forward is not to try to reproduce poor conditions artificially. There is something insulting to the really poor to boast of our simple life when we have comfortable shelter, adequate food and a large balance in the bank. Also the standard of what constitutes poverty varies enormously from one country to another. True spiritual poverty leads to liberality rather than a cult of economy. This is true whether we have much or little of this world's goods. John says that even on this material level we shall be happier and more fulfilled men and women without our possessiveness.

> Even if a man does not free his heart of joy in temporal goods for God . . . he ought to do so on account of the resulting temporal advantages. . . . By dismissing joy over temporal goods . . . he acquires the virtue of liber-

ality. Liberality is one of God's principal attributes and can in no way co-exist with covetousness. (*Ascent*, III.xx.2)

The poverty which leads to liberality is not extreme or ostentatious. It arises out of a grateful heart. Because God has supplied my needs I have something to share, and sharing is a happy thing even on a purely natural level. The more this spirit of giving is within us the more we shall trust and the less we shall worry.

Through this freedom we are given back God's gift of wonder, which we knew as children but lost as soon as we learned to manipulate people and things for our own ends. "He then whose joy is unpossessive of things rejoices in them all as though he possessed them all; another, beholding them with a possessive mind loses the satisfaction of them all in general" (*Ascent*, III.xx.3). Having read these words, can we still suspect John of being negative about life and creation as some people have suggested?

Without a cleansing of our greed and possessiveness we cannot even recognize other created beings for what they are, let alone supply their true needs. Covetousness blinds us to the reality and beauty of their little lives. But John says of a soul that is free,

In detachment from things he acquires a clearer knowledge of them so that he has a better understanding of both natural and supernatural truths concerning them. His joy, consequently, in these temporal goods . . . harmonizes with their truth, whereas that of the attached man is in accord with what is false in them. (*Ascent*, III.xx.2)

The "attached man" sees the ocean, for instance, only as a convenient garbage dump in which to drop his industrial waste. The detached person cherishes the sea and all that is in it for its own sake and for the sake of God who made it.

In the spirit of Romans 8 we now see humanity as God's high priest standing between earth and heaven, receiving his sacrament of the world and offering it back to him so that it too can fulfill its destiny. There need be no dichotomy between the things of earth and the things of heaven. Every renunciation of possession leaves the heart more free for God and, in him, for everything that he has made.

Joy in natural goods

Cf. *Ascent*, III.xxi; xxii.2; xxiii

> By natural goods we mean: beauty, grace, elegance, bodily constitution, and all other corporal endowments; also in the soul, good intelligence, discretion and other talents pertinent to the rational part of man. (*Ascent*, III.xxi.1)

While temporal goods indicate what we have, natural goods go far toward defining who we are. It is therefore difficult for us to accept that they too are gifts and not possessions which in some way do credit to ourselves. "A person is vain and deceitful," says John, "if he rejoices in these gifts only because he or his relations have them without giving thanks to God" (*Ascent*, III.xxii.1).

However, giving thanks is not enough. If we study John's list of natural gifts, sober truth will probably lead us to acknowledge that in due measure we have received some of them. Sometimes too we use them in the service of God. But we need to ask ourselves whether in fact our basic attitudes to these things are those of a steward or an owner. Do we use them as tools for getting our own way, as weapons for taking advantage of the less gifted, or as means for making life more pleasant for ourselves at the expense of others? John repeats that it is not the gifts themselves which are the trouble but our misuse of them. So we sense a note of exasperation in his voice as he says, "These natural graces and gifts are such a provocation and occasion both to the possessor and the beholder that there is scarcely a heart that escapes from this snare or bird-lime" (*Ascent*, III.xxi.1).

It is advisable for us to be modest about our advantages for the sake of others. "Whoever has these endowments should be careful and live cautiously lest through vain ostentation he be the occasion that someone withdraw his heart one iota from God" (*Ascent*, III.xxi.1).

If our hearts over-react spontaneously toward a person's beauty, charm, intelligence or sympathetic personality, we need to stand back a little and hold the relationship up to God. Otherwise we may find ourselves taking joy not in the truth of a person but in his or her window-dressing. Our whole attitude to reality becomes distorted through this misconception. Reason and judgement become clouded and our love for the things of God gradually fades. Comparison, which is nearly always divisive, enters in and takes the joy out of rejoicing.

> When the heart values one thing naturally, it turns from others on account of its concentration upon the esteemed object. . . . Such contempt may be internal, or may manifest itself externally through speech: this thing is not like that, or so and so is not like this person. (*Ascent*, III.xxii.2)

For instance, the birth of a new baby in the family may be a purely joyful event. But this joy will soon become tainted or even eroded if we are forever comparing him or her, either in envy or complacency, with the child down the road. Each birth is a unique creation of God; that is the true ground of our joy.

John tells us that the particular harm which results from joy in natural goods is "complacency, sensual delight and lusts." Relationships are broken. "On account of this joy we hear every day of many murders, lost reputations, insults, squandered fortunes, rivalries, quarrels, etc." (*Ascent*, III.xxii.3). John does not confine this to sexual attraction and desire but includes the many ways in which we are drawn to one person rather than another because they satisfy some need in us. Such love is self-centered, for we rarely stop to consider whether we ourselves are good for the one that we desire.

Next John comments on "flattery and vain praises which involve deception and vanity." We find it astonishing that tyrants and dictators of every age seem to have no notion of the falseness of the adulation which they receive, nor the self-preservation that prompts it. It is one thing to affirm a person's self-confidence by stressing their good points and quite another to attribute almost superhuman qualities where none exist. Not only dictators are subjected to these perverted expectations. Parents, for example, may insist that their children have gifts which are either greater or different from those they actually possess, and they will not be convinced otherwise. Then they are amazed and hurt at the resentment or depression shown by the child. Children, like all humans, want to be loved and accepted for who and what they are and deeply resent having to live a kind of prostitution in order to "earn" love and acceptance.

So John tells us that when we are free we shall be able to love others, not for their use to us, but as children of God in their own right. "In remaining unattached to everyone in spite of these apparent and deceptive natural goods, a person is unencumbered and free to love all rationally and spiritually, which is the way God wants him to love. . . . And when he loves with this motive, his love is according to God and exceedingly free" (*Ascent*, III.xxiii.1). This does not rule out a closer love for our families and friends, but if God comes first no one is harmed or left out. "If the love contains some attachment there is greater attachment to God, for as love of neighbor increases the love of God increases and vice versa" (*Ascent*, III.xxiii.1).

John says, "No one merits love except for his virtues." This is a difficult phrase for most of us. Yet it must be remembered that all human beings have virtue insofar as they are children of God, made in his image. Thus each of us, sinful though we may be, continues to receive the outpouring of God's love and grace. But in no way is love to be earned by good works. We ourselves have to believe in the divine spark within a soul even when we cannot see it, even as we believe that God continues to love us when we are utterly unlovable.

John speaks of other benefits that come to us through the redirecting of our joy to God. As our hearts and wills become purified by the influence of his love we may recognize that we are changing. Perhaps we have a new resistance to the temptations that bombard us through advertisements, some modern literature and the mass media. In our relationships with others, heart will find itself speaking simply to heart without the artificiality behind which we so often conceal ourselves. Then, John says, we shall be respected for what we truly are.

We cannot do all this by moral effort, but only by taking the living and loving God more completely into our hearts, so that the desire to live as he lived and love as he loves grows more strongly and effectively within us.

Joy in sensory goods

Cf. *Ascent*, III.xxiv-xxvi

> By sensory goods we mean all the goods apprehensible to the senses of sight, hearing, smell, taste and touch and to the interior faculty of discursive imagination. (*Ascent*, III.xxiv.1)

At the beginning of this section, John repeats one of the basic principles of his teaching, namely, that God in his essence can never be known through the senses or the imagination. Nevertheless the senses have a part to play in the gift of the whole person to God. Traces of his activity can be experienced through the senses "either from the spirit through some communication received interiorly from God, or from exterior things apprehended by them" (*Ascent*, III.xxiv.3). We see signs of his handiwork in the world and hear his voice through the voices of others. These things are meant to be pointers toward God. As John says, "There are souls who are greatly moved toward God by sensible objects" (*Ascent*, III.xxiv.4).

However, as we have seen, the senses cannot operate rightly until they are being purified in the active and passive nights. At this stage we may recognize that there has been a weakening of old compulsions and habits in our daily life. Yet unrecognized by ourselves our spirits may still be feeding on the sensory pleasure that prayer sometimes brings, rather than upon the darkness of faith which is its reality. If this is so we shall of course think we have lost God when the pleasurable experience dies away—as it always does. The true function of the senses in prayer is to trigger off the will toward God. In this they resemble the booster which falls away once the rocket is launched. Until this happens we are in danger of mistaking the pleasure for the prayer.

This is not easy to accept. In public worship, for example, it is often the sensory attraction of music or ritual which causes us to attend one church rather than another. Good liturgy itself is not God. It is only a pointer, a reminder or re-enactment of his presence. The reality is to be found just as truly in situations where there is no sensory excitement at all: in the sacrament celebrated by soldiers in the trenches, or in the intensive-care unit of a hospital. God is over and above and in all.

Some have deep experiences of God's presence in scenes of natural beauty; this was true of John himself. He recommends places for prayer "which have pleasant variations in the arrangement of the land and the trees and provide solitary quietude, all of which naturally awakens devotion" (*Ascent*, III.xlii.1). But he promptly adds that "it is advantageous to use these places [only] if one immediately directs the will to God in the forgetfulness of the place itself, since one should not be detained by the means and motive more than necessary for the attainment of the end" (ibid.).

There is a simple way of testing whether a sensory experience has brought us to God or whether it has been used merely as a means of release from strain or tension. In the gospels we read of Jesus and his disciples descending from the Mount of Transfiguration and immediately being confronted by a boy tormented by a devil (Lk 9:28-48). In the power of his transfiguration Jesus brought healing into that situation. So when we return to the market-place after an inspiring church service or a time of retreat, it is as well to note our reactions. Has the time on the mountain opened up and released our wellsprings of love for others, or are we irritated because our precious peace has so quickly been dispelled by their demands? John knew that the latter reaction was by no means unusual. "Frequently spiritual persons use this refreshment of the senses under the pretext of prayer and devotion to God; and they so perform these exercises that we could call this recreation rather than prayer, and the pleasing of self rather than God" (*Ascent*, III.xxiv.4).

In chapter xxv John lists the kind of harm "incurred by the desire for joy of will in sensory goods." This includes the distaste that we feel for things that are repugnant to our senses. The examples that John gives may not seem to be very relevant to our culture. For example, we do not readily equate "joy in sweet fragrance" with disgust for the poor or aversion to servants. Our sense of smell may rather be offended by the alcoholic, the cigarette smoker, the old or the sick. We shall not meet God in our ministry to such people if it is done out of a sense of duty, it is true, but with repugnance. Again we can look to Mother Teresa of Calcutta, who embraces the whole person, smell and all, before attending to their needs. In her sight they are all God's children, no matter what they look or smell or feel like.

So in contrast to the active night of sense we are not now speaking primarily of an ascetic exercise. We are involved in the whole contemplative movement of spirit whereby we bring all things to God. All people are our brothers and sisters in Christ no matter what our senses tell us about them. In *Ascent*, III.xxvi.5 we are told that as a result of this movement "the satisfaction and joy of the will is temporally and exceedingly increased, since, as the Savior says, in this life for one joy they will receive a hundredfold (Mk 10:30)."

We are promised that our purified senses will not die but find their true function and meaning in God. We discover in ourselves our own Eden, which God intended for us at our beginning. "In the state of innocence all that our first parents saw, spoke of and ate in the garden of paradise served them for more abundant delight in contemplation, since the sensory part of their souls was truly subjected and ordered to reason" (*Ascent*, III.xxvi.5).

To the pure all things are pure. Through redirection of our joy these goods become themselves a part of our contemplation rather than a hindrance to it. "Consequently, this person, now of pure heart, finds in all things a joyful, pleasant, chaste, pure, spiritual, glad, and loving knowledge of God" (*Ascent*, III.xxvi.6).

Joy in moral goods

Cf. *Ascent* III.xxvii-xxix

By moral goods we mean: the virtues and their habits insofar as they are moral; the exercise of any of the virtues; the practice of the works of mercy; the observance of God's law; urbanity and good manners. (*Ascent*, III.xxvii.1)

These qualities may be found in people of any religious persuasion and even in those of no religion at all. In contrast with the other kinds of joy which John describes, moral virtue is a good in itself apart from the use that we make of it. It brings peace and order into our minds so that we act consistently and with mature deliberation.

The scholastic theology of John's day recognized the reality of natural virtue, especially among the philosophers of the classical world. "God, who loves every good, even in the barbarian and gentile and does not hinder any good work from being accomplished . . . bestowed on them honor, dominion, and peace, besides an increase of life" (*Ascent*, III.xxvii.3). So on the walls of the painted monasteries of Romania we see Greek philosophers as well as Christian Fathers of the Church. The only difference is that the Christians have haloes while the pagan Greeks do not.

Today there is a diversity of ideas concerning the eternal destiny of the morally good who have not known Christ. We recognize that the great religions of the world such as Judaism and Islam also equate love of God with obedience to a moral code. We may question the medieval distinction between haloed Christian saints and other good persons. Yet whatever the relationship of God to his non-Christian children may be, it is their secret, not ours. Our secret, as Christians, is the great doctrine of justification by faith, which John is expounding in these chapters. We are not justified by natural virtue or good works but through faith in Christ.

Since the Christian has the light of faith, in which he hopes for eternal life, and without which nothing from above or below will have any value, he ought to rejoice

in the possession and exercise of these moral goods . . .
that insofar as he performs these works for the love of
God they procure eternal life for him. (*Ascent*, III.xxvii.4)

There are an infinite number of reasons, both religious and
non-religious, why people practice virtue rather than vice.
These include social pressure and fear of the law, self-interest
and ambition, and love of one's family, community or country.
These motives and others induce us to behave acceptably
whatever our religion may be. But for Christians they are all
subordinate to the one great desire that Christ may be formed
within them, that they should not, as it were, "abort" Christ
by conduct which denies his power within them. All human
motives, of course, are mixed. We often feel weighed down by
our sinfulness and yet keep on trying. It is in our oft-repeated
return to Christ in faith that we affirm him and reject the many
kinds of self-deception and hypocrisy to which we are prone.
So John's detailed analysis of the kinds of harm which stem
even from "joy in moral goods" need not be discouraging.

In chapter xxviii John first of all attacks self-righteousness
in all its forms. He points out the danger of measuring goodness by the standard of our own favorite moral principles. This
was not the way of Christ. In the gospels Jesus reaffirms the
great law of love of God and neighbor, but within these wide
limits his approach to human needs and questions is marked
by paradox. He brings peace but also a sword; he upholds the
Jewish law and yet plucks corn on the Sabbath day; he mourns
over the dead Lazarus whom he could have raised to life at
any time. The Pharisee in us wants black and white moral
absolutes by which we can judge ourselves and others. Instead
we are confronted by a living person whose Spirit directs us
in every circumstance of life. Obedience to his law of love may
sometimes seem to go against our most cherished principles—
as the disciples found in Galilee long ago.

Among the mixture of motives for doing good works is the

satisfaction that is found in doing them and pleasure in the credit we receive for our public spirit. It may be that as imperfect beings we need this encouragement when we find we are taken for granted, our free time is eroded and most of our work consists of unglamorous repetition. John however has little room for these lesser motives for joy. "There is so much misery in mankind as regards this kind of harm that I believe most of the works publicly achieved are either faulty, worthless, or imperfect in God's sight, because people are not detached from these human respects and interests" (*Ascent*, III.xxviii.5).

He is concerned lest, once the first interest diminishes, we produce nothing good or lasting, for our work is not done purely because God needs it. If we judge its objective value by the degree of personal fulfillment that we find in it, then our work is likely to be unreliable.

> Through this passion of joy the . . . appetites become so strong that they do not allow leeway for the judgement of reason. As a result a person usually becomes inconstant in his practice of good works and resolutions; he leaves these aside and takes up others, starting and stopping without ever finishing anything. (*Ascent*, III.xxix.2)

With this attitude it is difficult to accept constructive criticism and advice. Only too often, therefore, what begins with enthusiasm and generosity ends up in bitterness and recrimination. So John counsels us to aim for the highest motives in doing the right things.

Moral goodness will have a different quality once our eyes are fixed on Jesus rather than ourselves. Our actions will be more unobtrusive and less colored by our own egos. So God's power will have a greater freedom to work in us. "A wise man is concerned about the substance and profit of a work, not about the delight and satisfaction it yields. Thus he does not beat the air, but procures a stable joy" (*Ascent*, III.xxix.2). John uses words such as meekness, humility and prudence to describe such people. These qualities are often mistaken for weakness when in fact they are virtues of the strong. I know a judge who is not content merely to pass sentence across the void which divides him from the accused. He visits those he has sentenced to terms of community service at their place of work. He learns from them how they feel about it, whether the work given to them is worthwhile, how people behave toward them. He does not cling to his dignity but puts himself beside them. So he brings the compassion of Christ into the processes of the law.

We are very quick today to see through self-righteousness and hypocrisy, but true goodness still has its own attractiveness. It usually shows itself in a realism and humor about itself which disarms even the most critical. So John concludes by saying that by redirecting our joy in moral goodness to the God who gives it we become "pleasing to both God and man" (*Ascent*, III.xxix.5).

Joy in supernatural goods

Cf. *Ascent* III.xxx-xxxii

> By these we mean all the gifts and graces of God that exceed our natural faculties and powers. . . . Examples of these are the gifts of wisdom and knowledge God gave to Solomon and the graces Paul enumerates: faith, the grace of healing, working of miracles, prophecy, knowledge and discernment of spirits, interpretation of words and also the gift of tongues. (*Ascent*, III.xxx.1)

Notice first of all that John does not deny the reality of supernatural gifts. In fact they were common in the sixteenth century both within and outside the official Church, which regarded them with a careful but skeptical eye. John explains that while spiritual gifts are the means by which every soul can be brought into union with God, supernatural gifts are given for the service of other people. Certain of us receive some or all of them, but if we are not among that number we are none the worse as Christians.

John keeps very close to biblical teaching as he describes these gifts. He agrees that they can be a blessing as the sick are healed, devils are driven out and prophecies and warnings for the future are given. Yet what is important is the increase of love in those who do the works and those who see or benefit from them. Without this John does not think much of supernatural goods, since in themselves they do not unite us to God. Even wicked and godless persons have been known to work miracles. For as Paul says in 1 Corinthians 13:1, "I may have all knowledge and understanding; I may have all the faith needed to move mountains, but if I have no love I am nothing." When the disciples came back from their first mission rejoicing in their power to drive out devils, Jesus told them that they should rather rejoice that their names were written in heaven.

Supernatural gifts are dangerous in the hands of those who are unaware that they share the urge for power present in every human being. This may be fed by those clamoring to benefit from the special gifts of others. We all long for some short cut to get us out of our difficulties, apart from the slow, patient process of the cross. A favorite theme in fairy tales and children's comics is that of the magic talisman which when rubbed or invoked will produce instant solutions to every problem. We therefore tend to collude with those who possess charismatic gifts, encouraging them to use them on demand and not only when God wills it. Jesus, on the other hand, did not heal everyone in his country, and when he did the action was often costing and painful. John says that anyone rejoicing in their supernatural gifts as a possession is not fit to exercise them. "Due to his joy in the work, a man is not merely desirous of believing in it more quickly, but even impelled toward performing the work outside the proper time" (*Ascent,* III.xxxi.2). Even those with good will and judgement ought to use any unusual gifts they may possess with discretion. Such a person "should not desire or rejoice in its use, nor should he care about exercising it. God who grants the grace supernaturally for the utility of the Church or its members, will also move him supernaturally as to the manner and time in which he should use it" (*Ascent,* III.xxxi.7).

The threshold between using our gifts in obedience to God's prompting and using them on all occasions because we have them, is a narrow one. Nowhere is it more easy for the devil to masquerade as an angel of light. "Hence," says John, "we have wizards, enchanters, magicians, soothsayers and witches" (*Ascent,* III.xxxi.5). They are still with us today. As Christian faith declines so the old gods emerge to seduce us from obedience to Christ and his Church. Respectable bookshops sell works on the occult and astrology because of the demand for them. Despite our sophisticated culture we are still as vulnerable to the powers of natural religion as our ancestors were. We may be tempted to make a relationship with them outside of the God who made them and the incarnation which redeemed them. If we do we are in danger of arousing spirits over which we have no control and from which we have no natural protection.

John tells us that real faith may be lost or weakened if it becomes dependent on signs and miracles. A woman attending a prayer group had undergone eighteen operations on her knees and still they were not healed. She was told that if she had faith the prayers of the group together with the laying on of hands would cure her. We prayed diligently but the knees remained as bad as ever, in fact worse, as she demonstrated her faith by kneeling on them for communion. The suggestion that it was her own lack of belief that was at fault did not help.

A load of guilt was added to her other troubles. It is not surprising that in the end she felt that Christianity had little to offer her. But John tells us that real faith rests on something deeper than outward signs and for this reason God does not normally want miracles to be performed.

Let me repeat that John does recognize the place of charismatic gifts within the Church. As they appear in the New Testament, he can scarcely do otherwise. Probably it is his experience of their misuse which explains his reluctance to concede that they are one means, although not the greatest, for bringing souls to God. But, "The more faith and service rendered to God without testimonies and signs, the more extolment He receives from the soul, since it believes more of Him than what the signs and miracles can teach" (*Ascent*, III.xxxii.3).

Joy in spiritual goods

Cf. *Ascent* III.xxxiii; xxxix; xlv

> I refer by spiritual goods to all those that are an aid and motivating force in turning the soul to divine things and to converse with God, as well as a help in God's communications to the soul. (*Ascent*, III.xxxiii.2)

John is so conscious of the many kinds of spiritual goods that are open to us that twelve chapters of *The Ascent* are not enough to describe them. He divides and subdivides them into those that are pleasant and those that are painful; those we can recognize immediately to be good and those that are vague and obscure; and those that are associated with the memory, the intellect and the will. The second book of *The Dark Night of the Soul* is concerned with the "painful goods." Here in *The Ascent* John writes of some of the "delightful goods that are clear and distinct." Even so, we only possess part of what he meant to write, because Book III of *The Ascent* ends abruptly halfway through chapter xlv.

John's main purpose is to show us how religious practice should feed our personal love for God. As Evangelicals frequently remind us, the former is useless without the latter. Without the direction of the heart Godward the practice and politics of religion will weaken our faith rather than strengthen it.

As a faithful Spanish Catholic of the sixteenth century, John does not condemn the use of statues, rosaries, special devotions and holy places in themselves. However, he spells out how they should be used and what should be avoided if they are to draw the soul to the invisible God. As he says, their effectiveness does not depend on their beauty and elaborateness but on their power to enkindle the prayer of the heart.

Although the décor of most churches is more simple today, we have no grounds for feeling superior. Every denomination has its own cherished customs and aids to worship. Particular language and forms of service, hymns, posture during prayer (Presbyterians sit, Episcopalians kneel), all help to establish our identity. This in itself is no bad thing. Through these loved and familiar actions and objects our beings are drawn Godward, and so John speaks of them as "a possible object of joy for the will." Yet if we become deeply disturbed over minor changes in ritual, music or language in our local church we ought to question our motives. Are we becoming dependent on the décor rather than the substance of worship? Are we seeking entertainment or security in familiarity? A new thing may not necessarily be better, but we cannot know until we have opened ourselves to it.

John moves on to discuss the place of hearing rather than sight in worship. Only words spoken from the heart can convert. "For the living Spirit enkindles fire . . . good style, gestures, sublime doctrine and well-chosen words" all help, but unless the spirit is on fire the will "will ordinarily be left as weak and remiss as before, even though wonderful things were admirably spoken; and the sermon merely delights the sense of hearing, like a musical concert or sounding bells" (*Ascent*, III.xlv.4). Something is needed from the listeners too. As they sit down to their Sunday dinners they may speak appreciatively of the sermon and even repeat its points. But unless the message is practiced during the rest of the week, hearing sermons may also become an entertainment and form of idolatry.

John's teaching on the practice of the active night of spirit in every area of life can provide a program for daily living. In it the nitty-gritty of discipleship is worked out as we gradually discover our freedom in Christ. But the six focal points for our joy, hope, grief and fear which John has discussed can never be seen in isolation from each other. They are bound together in the individual who is a single organism, not a collection of bits and pieces. It is the whole person who is in the process of change as the intellect, memory and will become infused with faith, hope and charity. It is a long process, and we can never claim to have achieved our end in this life. John tells us that now the soul usually spends many years in exercising itself in the state of proficients. "In this new state, as in one liberated from a cramped prison cell, the soul goes about the things of God with much more freedom and satisfaction of spirit and with more abundant interior delight than it did in the beginning" (*Night*, II.i.1).

Nevertheless life in this world will always have its shadows. Even at this stage John warns us of "certain needs, aridities, darkness and conflicts" which will disturb our peace. We shall experience our problems, losses, sicknesses and disappointments. Nevertheless our darkness at this stage will not torment us for too long. "Thus God purges some individuals who are not destined to ascend to as lofty a degree of love as are others. He brings them into this night of contemplation and spiritual purgation at intervals, frequently causing the night to come and then the dawn" (*Night*, II.i.1). At present our soul is too weak to bear strong infusions of God's Spirit. Sometimes this affects the body. John regards rapture and excitement as a weakness which will be burnt out in the passive night of spirit and be replaced by the darkness of faith.

For some these transitory experiences of darkness may be an omen or messenger of a deeper night of spirit to come. We can neither desire nor evade it if God brings us to this place. It is not esoteric, for it is open to all who are willing to let God do his work within them. If we are among this number we ought not to be surprised if he takes us at our word and helps us to achieve our desire through what John calls "painful goods."

This is the subject of the second book of *The Dark Night of the Soul*, and even if the subjects he discusses are outside our experience at this point, it may not always be so. It will help us then to know that they are a part of the common mystical experience of the Church, and that we are not alone in our suffering and darkness. Above all we shall know the companionship of the cross without which, John believes, there can be no true joy of sense and spirit.

7

The Passive Night of Spirit

Darkness

Cf. *The Dark Night of the Soul* II. ii; iv; v

As we have already seen, the nights of spirit form a large part of our sharing in the cross. In the active night the cross will never be far away if our joy in God is to contain and take precedence over other joys. We carry it through life as gently and steadily as we can, picking it up again whenever we let it fall through sin, negligence or weakness. Here we are, to a certain extent, in control. It is our decision whether or not we act in accordance with our Christian faith or according to our immediate reactions and desires. In the passive night of spirit, however, we find ourselves nailed to a cross which we probably have not chosen. Our only choice lies in whether we bear it in the spirit of the repentant or the unrepentant thieves who were both crucified with Jesus.

In the nights of sense we learned a degree of acceptance of what was done to us. Now, however, God is piercing deeper into the unconverted places of the soul, which are well known to him if not to us.

The difference between the two purgations is like the

difference between pulling up roots and cutting off a
branch, or rubbing out a fresh stain and an old, deeply
embedded one. If these are not wiped away by the use
of the soap and strong lye of this purgative night, the
spirit will be unable to reach the purity of divine union.
(*Night,* II.i.2)

For John the whole process is one of mature love. It is a special
kind of passivity that he recommends, one which arises out of
this love and trust. Nevertheless, as we read chapter v and
those that follow, we may well believe that he is describing a
psychological condition rather than a spiritual night. In some
cases the symptoms may be similar. In fact, it is not the degree
of pain which is the deciding factor but our attitude within it.
In psychological sickness there is often a fear of being incapa-
ble of love and a belief that one is not lovable. In the passive
night of spirit we cling to the hope that it is love that has
brought us to this place and love that will hold us in it. Our
place is to stay with the situation, hoping against hope. "In the
midst of these dark and loving afflictions, the soul feels the
presence of someone and an interior strength which so forti-
fies and accompanies it that when this weight of anxious
darkness passes, it often feels alone, empty and weak" (*Night,*
II.xi.7). The power of God is within the pressure, not in spite
of it.

A psychological state of anxiety, depression or paranoia is
often undifferentiated, spreading itself impartially over whatever life may bring. We may be conscious only of paralysis in
the face of its demands; every person may seem to threaten
our frail security. But this is a false picture of reality, which in
fact is sometimes life-giving and sometimes hostile. In the
passive night of spirit, sense and spirit are purified in and
through concrete situations. We may have negative feelings
about our experiences, but these are not a sign of sickness if
they are appropriate to the objective situation. If we read

chapters v-viii in the context of John's sufferings in his Toledo prison, we cannot feel that his comments are exaggerated or paranoic. It would in fact have been more abnormal had he not let himself acknowledge his suffering and sense of abandonment.

The passive night of spirit is not as exalted and unusual as we may hope. It must inevitably touch the lives of many Christians who are growing into maturity of love. At some time in our lives most of us experience situations in which we seem to be fixed and which may seem almost intolerable. Their context may be commonplace: a marriage, our family, our work, a prolonged illness, even for some a long prison sentence. Most of us will come to know the tedious deprivations and frustrations of old age. As we plod on as positively as we can, we may not even realize that we are in this night until a sudden ray of light pierces the darkness. The cloud lifts for a moment and we see something of its value and meaning. John tells us that although the intensity of suffering is only felt at intervals, the night itself may last for some years if it is to do its work properly. "As fire consumes the tarnish and rust of metal, this contemplation annihilates, empties and consumes all the affections and imperfect habits the soul contracted throughout its life" (*Night*, II.vi.5). John says that this work will go on just as long as necessary.if we are to become one with the Spirit of God according to the desire of love that God in his mercy desires to grant. We may ask what "this contemplation" is that he mentions, for it may seem to us that prayer is impossible. But our faith now rests in God's continual contemplation of us. We know that we are the subject of his prayer and work, and we affirm this even in the midst of our darkness. This is the umbilical cord that holds us to him.

John himself does not go into details about the sources of impurity and weakness which have brought us into this state. These need not necessarily be of our own making. Our flawed nature is affected by the wounds of the world as a whole or by those around us. We cannot know how much of our thoughts and feelings, our opinions and moral values are affected by world pressure, for we are all bound together in the bundle of life. A young French nun, Thérèse of Lisieux, discovered this as she lay dying. She experienced as her own the disbelief and materialism of French society at the end of the nineteenth century. "It is a wall that reaches up to heaven," she cried. "God has disappeared." Yet because her faith was rooted in Christ's offering rather than her own, she found peace and serenity at the end.

Let us also not forget the pressures of the natural world around us, that world for which we are the priests and the servants. "For the creation waits with eager longing for the revealing of the sons of God" (Rom 8:19). In the night of the great storm in South-East England in 1987 I awoke early in the morning in a state of terror for which there seemed no explanation in the quiet cottage in Donegal where I was then living. Danger seemed near, yet, as I afterward found, it was others' danger, not my own, that I was sensing. In the love-bond within the Body of Christ it is not surprising that we should sometimes know these things, even though it is as well not to make too much of them.

Whatever cross we are crucified on, whether it be one of our own or someone else's making, does not ultimately matter. What does matter is that we do not try to bear it alone, for it is a part of Christ's cross and that of suffering creation. His life is ours and our pain is his when borne in solidarity with everyone else's. It is there that we find joy at the heart of darkness.

Darkness and light

Night, II.vii.4 and 6; viii.4 and 5; ix.1, 6, 9-11

In these scattered passages we discover that John is not threatening us with a life of unmitigated darkness. The sun breaks unexpectedly through the fog from time to time.

> There are intervals in which this dark contemplation ceases to assail the soul in a purgative mode and shines upon it illuminatively and lovingly. Then the soul, like one who has been unshackled and released from a dungeon and who can enjoy the benefits of spaciousness and freedom, experiences great sweetness of peace and loving relationship with God. (*Night*, II.vii.4)

John says that this illumination is for the soul a sign of increasing health and a foretaste of good things to come. In this light we see something of the reason for our darkness and what more it has to do within us. John uses, as he did in *The Ascent*, the image of a ray of sunlight shining through a room, visible only because of the dust through which it passes. The light shows up the particles.

> When this spiritual light finds an object on which to shine, that is, when something is to be understood spiritually concerning perfection or imperfection, no matter how slight, or about a judgement on the truth or falsity of some matter, a man will understand more clearly than he did before he was in darkness. (*Night*, II.viii.4)

However, dust consists of many particles. When we are in the light we believe that darkness will never come again, unaware as we are of the deeper layers of sin and imperfection within us. So we are thrust back into the night and forget the freedom we have been enjoying. Now it seems that the darkness will never end. These alternations between light and darkness will continue until the whole self is purified. "For until the spiritual purification is completed . . . the soul does not cease to feel that something is lacking or remaining to be done. . . . . It feels as though an enemy is within it who, although pacified and put to sleep, will awaken and cause trouble" (*Night*, II.vii.6). As John says, this is most likely to happen when we feel safest and least expect it.

It is not a fairly top-level experience that can serve to purify us now but rather the "dark contemplation" in which we accept it. For instance, a long-drawn-out illness or a court order may lead to a ban on driving, perhaps for some years. On the superficial, sensual level we shall experience considerable inconvenience and frustration. When the ban is lifted it will feel as if we have emerged into daylight. We may likewise have learned greater care and consideration for the future. But below the surface God will have been working through the experience upon deeper fears and angers of which we were probably unaware. Fear of dependence on others or resentment of restraint are not little things. But until God gives us the light to name them and offer them, we may only perceive them as a weight of depression or anger. This will lift more readily if, like the good thief on the cross, we can accept the burden with as much faith and love as possible. Fighting against the pain will only make it worse; we need a non-violent response to ourselves as well as others.

So it may be in our deeper darknesses. Our contemplation rests on words of holy scripture: "My grace is sufficient for you, for my power is made perfect in weakness" (2 Cor 12:9); "God is faithful, and he will not let you be tempted beyond your strength, but with the temptation will also provide the way of escape that you may be able to endure it" (1 Cor 10:13). When God lifts his hand we can see the positive side of what has been unrelieved nuisance or misery. We find that pain is not an enemy in itself when we begin to treat it as a friend. As we see in the passion of Our Lord, he did not withdraw himself in the face of suffering and enmity. He was concerned for those who crucified him, for his mother and the penitent thief. He expressed his needs, he protested to the Father about his treatment, but nevertheless died with words of trust on his lips. And we know how powerful and effective the cross still is when it is really displayed in the lives of Christians.

We are challenged by Christ to exercise our love in absorbing evil, letting it stop with us, rather than spreading it. I remember an ecumenical service in the Anglican cathedral in Belfast, at which Cardinal Suenens had been invited to speak. Scarcely had he begun his address when small groups of protesters rose up in turn to drown his words. Nevertheless he serenely continued, although no one could hear what he said. Only at the end, when the tumult had died down, did we hear him praying in a gracious and friendly manner for love and joy for ourselves and our opponents. The standing ovation he received indicated the power of his witness to a non-violence which was not appeasement, cowardice or *laissez-faire*. It was the simple and loving acceptance of suffering for reconciliation.

John wonders why we make so much fuss about suffering when the results to be obtained from it can be so great. "How amazing and pitiful it is that . . . the hand of God, though light and gentle, should feel so heavy and contrary. For the hand of God does not press down or weigh upon the soul, but only touches it; and this mercifully, for God's aim is to grant it favors and not chastise it" (*Night*, II.v.7). In chapter ix he asks why the light of contemplation should at first have such disagreeable effects, since it is for this that we were born. He gives three reasons. The first lies in the weakness of our souls and bodies to bear the weight of the Spirit; the second in our inadequate preparation in the active nights; and the third in our lack of understanding of the greatness of God's gift and that which prevents us from receiving it.

But John says that this will not always be so. Those rays of light which are given to us are a foretaste of the joy and fulfillment which will be ours. We sense this when God lifts his hand from us in compassion, but his real work is done in secret and in darkness.

The log and the fire

Cf. *Night*, II.x; xi.1-3

> The very loving light and wisdom into which the soul will be transformed is that which in the beginning purges and prepares it, just as the fire which transforms the wood by incorporating it into itself is that which was first preparing it for this transformation. (*Night*, II.x.3)

This is the second of John's illustrations of the whole inner journey. Here we see the log being acted upon by the fire as the soul is worked upon by God. This image contrasts with that of the map of Mount Carmel, in which the soul ascends at least in part by its own efforts in the active nights. No single illustration can embrace the richness and variety of God's ways with us. Yet through darkness and light, activity and passivity, it is the same God of love who works unceasingly to draw us to himself.

John compares us to logs which are made of good natural material capable of being transformed. With a decision which has to be repeated many times, we lay ourselves open to the fire's action. Some of us are drier logs to start with and more ready to respond to the flame. Some of us are drier at one point of our lives than we are at others. Others of us are damp and mossy, full of romantic ideas, perhaps, and looking for security and thrills in religion. What is real is dried out from the dampness of illusion before the fire can take hold. As the wood dries, the flame pierces further inward and the creepy-crawlies which have been living deep within come running out. These are the "ugly and dark accidents which are contrary to fire." My dictionary tells me that the word "accident" used in this sense is an "attribute which is not part of the essence." In essence we are the children of God, made in his image, and the fire banishes only what is contrary to that reality. We mistakenly think that these "accidents" are our real self and so feel blackened and ruined, although, as John says, in reality we are no worse than we were before. Now, finding no resistance, the flame burns ever brighter, transforming the log into itself. The wood begins to live with the life of the fire rather than its own.

> Once transformed the wood no longer has any activity or passivity of its own, except for its weight and quantity which is denser than the fire. For it possesses the properties and performs the actions of fire: it is dry and it dries; it is hot and it gives off heat; it is brilliant and it illumines; and it is also light, much lighter than before. It is the fire that produces all these properties in the wood. (*Night*, II.x.1)

John then summarizes the benefits that the fire has bestowed on the soul, which we have already discussed. And we can almost hear the sigh of relief with which he tells us that "it will be a good thing to leave these sad experiences and begin now to discuss the fruit of the soul's tears and the happy traits about which it begins to sing" (*Night*, II.x.10). We are transformed by God's love for us rather than our feeble love for him. All we can do is give our consent and try to keep our whole being open to his action.

Our sensory and spiritual joy has now a different quality

than it had before. We are not so conscious of what we are doing, thinking and feeling in relation to God. "Since this love is infused, it is more passive than active and thus generates in the soul a strong passion of love" (*Night*, II.xi.2). We become clearly aware that in our relationship God is the subject and we are the object. If we accept this we find it easier to co-operate with what he is doing with us. "This love is now beginning to possess something of union with God and thereby shares to a certain extent in its properties. These properties are actions of God more than of the soul and they reside in it passively, although the soul does give its consent" (*Night*, II.xi.2).

Chapters xv-xxiv of this book consist of a commentary on the second stanza of John's poem on *The Dark Night*:

> In darkness and secure,
> By the secret ladder, disguised,
> —Ah, the sheer grace!—
> In darkness and concealment,
> My house being now all stilled.

John's image has now changed. We come out of the fire into the freedom of the children of God. In fact we find ourselves on the heights of Mount Carmel where "only the honor and glory of God dwells." We have returned to what we were meant to be when God created us. John's language is now startling.

This renovation is an illumination of the human intellect with supernatural light so that it becomes divine, united with the divine; an informing of the will with love of God so that it is no longer less than divine and loves in no other way than divinely, united and made one with the divine love . . . . And thus this soul will be a soul of heaven, heavenly and more divine than human. (*Night*, II.xiii.11)

We have to turn to another of John's works to put this

extravagant language into proportion. "Although the substance of this soul is not the substance of God, since it cannot undergo a substantial conversion into Him, it has become God through participation in God, being united to and absorbed in Him as it is in this state" (*The Living Flame of Love*, Commentary on Stanza 2.34).

The end of our pilgrimage lies in nothing less than the divinization of our human creaturely nature. It is the glimpses of this that we encounter on the way which encourage us to be "drier wood" for the flame of God's love to burn and transform.

Interlude

The Secret Ladder of Love

Cf. *Night*, II.xviii-xxi

The image of a ladder to describe the complete journey of the soul Godward is a common one among spiritual writers. The ten steps which John describes are taken from earlier writers, but he has his own way of interpreting them. His approach, for instance, is very different from that of a medieval icon of the ladder of John Climacus which I possess. This is painted for the edification of monks. They are seen struggling up a ladder to the place at the top where Christ and his angels wait to welcome them. At every stage some fall off to be captured by devils and pitchforked into hell. It is a win-all, lose-all situation, and although Christ awaits the victors he is not on the ladder with them.

John's image represents Jacob's ladder on which there is continual ascent and descent. Also it has to be seen in the context of the many other images which he uses in the poem of *The Dark Night*. In response to the call of the Bridegroom, the soul as the Bride goes out from her house by a secret ladder, but we do not know whether she ascends or descends it. In chapter xviii we are told that she does both, as she looks upward to the transcendent God and downward to her human condition. "For on this road to descend is to ascend and to ascend is to descend, since he who humbles himself is exalted and he who exalts himself is humbled" (*Night*, II.xviii.2).

Although in chapters xix and xx John describes the increase of love in terms of ascending progress, yet in common speech we say that love deepens as it draws nearer to its object. This is also true of our love for God who, though present everywhere, is present to us only in the depths of our being. So it is reasonable to think of the soul descending into itself with increasing love to find the incarnate Christ who has all the time been drawing us. It is true that we shall probably find darkness, frustration and even despair in the course of our descent. We may feel that devils are throwing us off the ladder. Yet below it all we may hope to find God walking in the garden of our humanity as he walked with Adam and Eve in the dawn of creation.

So as we consider these ten steps, let it not be in any cut-and-dried fashion. If we take them as they stand in terms of ascent, we may be aware that one step up is often followed by two steps down. Or perhaps we feel that we have stood on one rung for years, unable to take the upward step which is needed and yet unwilling to sink lower. The progress which John describes can only be a general movement Godward in which there are as many ramifications as there are persons. So let us consider these ten steps in that light.

1. Our journey begins when the good as well as the bad things of life begin to lose their attraction. The soul "becomes unable to find satisfaction, support, consolation, or a resting place in anything" (*Night*, II.xix.1). We feel that there must be a deeper meaning to life. John says that this restlessness is a sign that God is calling us closer to himself.

2. We begin to search for God seriously, looking for signs of his presence in all things and at all times through the use of our active powers and senses. This is a time of spiritual convalescence.

3. Now we feel an intense desire to serve God. No matter how much we do, it never seems enough, and so we compare ourselves unfavorably with other people. "A person thinks inwardly that he is really worse than all others . . . conscious that his work is so lowly for so high a Lord" (*Night,* II.xix.3). This is the exaggerated zeal of the beginner which is going to be tested to the full as we try to follow the Christian way.

4. Here we experience suffering, even though "love makes all burdensome and heavy things nearly nothing." We experience difficulty and pain in bringing the flesh under the control of the spirit in the nights of sense. "Spiritually speaking, the desert is an interior detachment from every creature in which the soul neither pauses nor rests in anything" (*Night,* II.xix.4).

5. Freed from some of our more superficial attachments and addictions, we are impatient to achieve that union with God which would be our reward. But our human nature is still too weak and frail to be able to bear the direct touch of God upon it.

6. Through the nights of spirit we gain strength of body and charity of soul. Now we are more capable of responding to God's direct action upon us.

7. These touches of God fill us with "ardent boldness" and freedom to respond unhesitantly to his commands and invitations. "At this stage love neither profits by the judgement to wait nor makes us of the counsel to retreat, neither can it be curbed through shame" (*Night,* II.xx.2).

8. We are beginning to experience what union with God will mean but "the soul rests on it for only short periods of time" (*Night,* II.xx.3).

9. Here our union with God is as close and habitual as it can be in this life.

10. "The tenth and last step of this secret ladder of love assimilates the soul to God completely because of the clear vision of God which a person possesses as soon as he reaches it" (*Night*, II.xx.5). We shall know this only in the life to come when we may hope to share freely in God's life of love which is the Trinity.

If the deepening nights mark the increasing stringency of our purification, the ladder shows us the matching growth in love. These are the two aspects of one movement into union with God. We cannot judge accurately at any given moment where we are on the ladder; only as we look back can we see something of the way we have trodden. Even so, the whole pattern will only reveal itself as we stand on the tenth step after this life and see in God what he has done in us. Even now, however, we may find encouragement in terms of increasing health or freedom or love without defining their quantity or quality too closely.

So faith, hope and love are the necessary armor for our progress into an unknown future. As our intellects, memories and wills gradually become transfused with these virtues, we recognize that our inner world is changing. The "white tunic of faith" becomes our protection against the wiles of the devil, whose weapons are argument and confusion. Over this we put the "green coat of mail," which is hope protecting us from the seductions of the world. The "red cloak of charity" covers everything and protects us from the temptations of the flesh. "For where there is true love of God, love of self and of one's own things finds no entry" (*Night*, II.xxi.10).

This is the ideal, which will not be fully attained in this life, according to John. But in the measure to which we do approach it God will use what we are, however poor and humble, for the healing and transformation of the world.

8

The Way of Union

The Spiritual Canticle (2d Redaction)

Bride

1. Where have you hidden,
   Beloved and left me moaning?
   You fled like the stag
   After wounding me;
   I went out calling You, and You were gone.

2. Shepherds, you that go
   Up through the sheepfolds to the hill,
   If by chance you see
   Him I love most,
   Tell him that I sicken, suffer and die.

3. Seeking my Love
   I will head for the mountains and for watersides,
   I will not gather flowers,
   Nor fear wild beasts;
   I will go beyond strong men and frontiers.

4. O woods and thickets
   Planted by the hand of my beloved!
   O green meadow,

148

Coated, bright with flowers.
Tell me, has He passed by you?

5. Pouring out a thousand graces,
    He passed these groves in haste;
    And having looked at them,
    With His image alone,
    Clothed them in beauty.

6. Ah, who has power to heal me?
    Now wholly surrender yourself!
    Do not send me
    Any more messengers,
    They cannot tell me what I must hear.

7. All who are free
    Tell me a thousand graceful things of You;
    All wound me more
    And leave me dying
    Of, ah, I don't-know-what behind their **stammering.**

8. How do you endure
    O life, not living where you live?
    And being brought near death
    By the arrows you receive
    From that which you conceive of your **Beloved.**

9. Why, since You wounded
    This heart, don't You heal it?
    And why, since You stole it from me,
    Do You leave it so,
    And fail to carry off what You have stolen?

10. Extinguish these miseries,
    Since no one else can stamp them out;
    And may my eyes behold You
    Because You are their light,
    And I would open them to You alone.

11. Reveal Your presence,
     And may the vision of Your beauty be my death;
     For the sickness of love
     Is not cured
     Except by Your very presence and image.

12. O spring like crystal!
     If only, on your silvered-over face,
     You would suddenly form
     The eyes I have desired
     Which I bear sketched deep within my heart.

13. Withdraw them, Beloved,
     I am taking flight!

     Bridegroom

     Return, dove,
     The wounded stag
     Is in sight on the hill,
     Cooled by the breeze of your flight.

Bride

14. My Beloved is the mountain,
     And lonely wooded valleys,
     Strange islands,
     And resounding rivers,
     The whistle of love-stirring breezes.

15. The tranquil night
     At the time of the rising dawn,
     Silent music,
     Sounding solitude,
     The supper that refreshes, and deepens love.

16. Catch us the foxes,
     For our vineyard is now in flower,
     While we fashion a cone of roses

Intricate as the pine's
And let no one appear on the hill.

17. Be still, deadening north wind;
South wind come, you that awaken love,
Breathe through my garden,
Let its fragrance flow,
And the Beloved will feed amid the
flowers.

18. You girls of Judea,
While among flowers and roses
The amber spreads its perfume,
Stay away, there on the outskirts:
Do not so much as seek to touch our thresholds.

19. Hide Yourself, my love;
Turn Your face toward the mountains,
And do not speak;
But look at those companions
Going with her through strange islands.

Bridegroom

20. Swift-winged birds,
Lions, stags and leaping roes,
Mountains, lowlands and river banks,
Waters, winds and ardors,
Watching fears of night:

21. By the pleasant lyres
And the siren's song, I conjure you
To cease your anger
And not touch the wall,
That the bride may sleep in deeper peace.

22. The bride has entered
The sweet garden of her desire,

And she rests in delight,
Laying her neck
On the gentle arms of her Beloved.

23. Beneath the apple tree:
There I took you for My own,
There I offered you My hand,
And restored you,
Where your mother was corrupted.

Bride

24. Our bed is in flower,
Bound round with linking dens of lions,
Hung with purple,
Built up in peace,
And crowned with a thousand shields of gold.

25. Following Your footprints
Maidens run along the way;
The touch of a spark
The spiced wine,
Cause flowings in them from the balsam of God.

26. In the inner wine cellar
I drank of my Beloved and, when I went abroad
Through all this valley
I no longer knew anything,
And lost the herd which I was following.

27. There He gave me his breast;
There He taught me a sweet and living knowledge;
And I gave myself to Him,
Keeping nothing back;
There I promised to be His bride.

28. Now I occupy my soul
And all my energy in His service;

I no longer tend the herd,
Nor have I any other work
Now that my every act is love.

29. If, then, I am no longer
Seen or found on the common,
You will say that I am lost;
That, stricken by love,
I lost myself and was found.

30. With flowers and emeralds
Chosen on cool mornings
We shall weave garlands
Flowering in your love,
And bound with one hair of mine.

31. You considered
That one hair fluttered at my neck;
You gazed at it upon my neck;
And it captivated You;
And one of my eyes wounded You.

32. When You looked at me
Your eyes imprinted Your grace in me;
For this You loved me ardently;
And thus my eyes deserved
To adore what they beheld in You.

33. Do not despise me;
For if, before, You found me dark,
Now truly You can look at me
Since You have looked
And left in me grace and beauty.

Bridegroom

34. The small white dove
Has returned to the ark with an olive branch;

And now the turtledove
Has found its longed-for mate
By the green river banks.

35. She lived in solitude,
And now in solitude has built her nest;
And in solitude He guides her,
He alone, who also bears
In solitude the wound of love.

Bride

36. Let us rejoice, Beloved,
And let us go forth to behold ourselves in Your beauty,
To the mountain and to the hill,
To where the pure water flows,
And further, deep into the thicket.

37. And then we will go on
To the high caverns in the rock
Which are so well concealed;
There we shall enter
And taste the fresh juice of the pomegranates.

38. There You will show me
What my soul has been seeking,
And then You will give me,
You, my Life, will give me there
What You gave me on that other day:

39. The breathing of the air,
The song of the sweet nightingale,
The grove and its living beauty
In the serene night,
With a flame that is consuming and painless.

40. No one looked at her,
Nor did Aminadab appear;

The siege was still;
And the cavalry,
At the sight of the waters, descended.

The hidden God

Cf.   *Canticle*, Prologue; stanzas 1-21
      John's commentary on these stanzas

We now come to John's greatest poem in which he expresses the relationship of God with the human soul in all its richness and diversity. Within it we may recognize his ways with us through our own faith-history. For each of us the drama is intensely personal as it is acted out within the depths of our being.

Oh then, soul, most beautiful among all His creatures, so anxious to know the dwelling-place of your Beloved that you may go in quest of Him and be united with Him, now we are telling you that you yourself are His dwelling and His secret chamber and hiding place. This is something of immense gladness for you. (Commentary on Stanza 1.7)

John does not spend much time on the preliminaries, for he is more interested in the life of union after the nights of sense and spirit have done their work. He does not even mention them by name here. This poem has its own prologue addressed to a Carmelite nun, Mother Anne of Jesus. He tells her that the verses of *The Spiritual Canticle* were written out of a fullness of love that can only be understood through the reader's own experience. Therefore, "It is better to explain the utterances of love in their broadest sense so that each one may derive profit from them according to the mode and capacity of his spirit" (Prologue to *The Spiritual Canticle*).

The whole work, in common with the biblical Song of Songs on which it is modelled, is a love poem. Whether we are male or female in gender our soul is feminine toward God. He is the eternal Bridegroom who draws the soul toward himself as his Bride. Whatever stage we may be at, it is a part of one whole progress. We shall find hints of the end even in the beginning, and the need for watchfulness is never absent even in the unitive way.

Now we shall follow the Christian soul as she sets out upon her pilgrim way. Two versions of this poem have come down to us, and both are known to be John's own work. Here we shall follow the second version or redaction, in which the order of verses has been revised and an extra one (stanza 11) added.

In the introduction to John's commentary on the first stanza we are told that the soul has arrived at the point of decision. She has been meditating on holy scripture, the shortness of life, and God's goodness to her, and her desire for him has been awakened. Very soon she begins to experience touches of his love, which pierce her with a consciousness of her separation and incompleteness without him. The first twelve stanzas of the poem cover the initial stages of her journey in search of him.

Stanza 3 corresponds to the active night of sense. There are high mountains which have to be traversed, the seduction of sweet-smelling flowers to be avoided, wild beasts to be conquered and frontiers to be passed. Firm action is needed here.

In stanzas 4-7 she seeks for God among the beauties and wonders of the created world. But these soon cease to satisfy her, for their message is stammering and incomplete. "Do not send me / Any more messengers, / They cannot tell me what I must hear" (stanza 6). This represents the passive night of sense in which meditation gives place to silence. Only God himself will do.

John passes on quickly to stanzas 8-11, to the conflict and tension involved in the active night of spirit. The soul is struggling to bring her life in this world into conformity with life in God.

Stanza 12 is a transitional point leading on to the passive night of spirit. Within herself the soul senses the eternal spring of hope. It spreads out into a still pool which is, however, "silvered-over" so that she can see only through the eyes of dark faith. In this darkness God himself is purifying her, although she cannot see him.

Stanzas 13-21 describe the period of closer engagement or "spiritual espousals" which precedes complete union. In stanza 13 the soul still experiences the suffering caused by the impact of the Spirit upon the weak flesh. She tries to escape from this through ecstasy but is soon brought back to the realities of her incarnate condition. Stanzas 14 and 15 speak of a more solid joy which begins to transform the things of the earth. God is communicating something of his own life so that moral goodness no longer appears unnatural or difficult. Sometimes this life flows over her overwhelmingly like flood-water from "resounding rivers." Sometimes it comes like a whisper of the first dawn-breeze in the depths of night. The ways of God with the soul are rich and varied. Creation itself has now become a sign and sacrament of God.

> The soul perceives in that tranquil wisdom that all creatures, higher and lower ones alike, according to what each in itself has received from God, raise their voice in testimony to what God is. She beholds that each in its own way, hearing God within itself according to its capacity, magnifies God. And thus all these voices form one voice of music praising the grandeur, wisdom, and wonderful knowledge of God. (*Canticle*, Commentary on Stanza 15.27)

Yet there still is not undisturbed peace. The soul is tormented by the "little foxes" of sensual temptations as we see in stanza

16, but instead of fighting against them she takes refuge in the living Christ within. Joy and suffering are intensified in stanzas 17-19. The dryness of the "deadening north wind" becomes even harder to bear, and the Holy Spirit comes to the relief of the sufferer in the form of the refreshing southern breeze.

In stanza 19 the soul says that she is no longer satisfied with an indirect knowledge and communication of God through effects and works but longs for a direct contact of heart and heart. John says, "This communication is not brought about through any means, but through a certain contact of the soul with the divinity. This contact is something foreign to everything sensory and accidental, since it is a touch of naked substances—of the soul and the divinity" (Commentary on Stanza 19.4). Finally, there must be an assent by the soul to the Bridegroom before the spiritual espousals can flower into spiritual marriage. "The Bride . . . must hold the door of her will open to the Bridegroom that He may enter through the complete and true 'yes' of love" (Commentary on Stanza 20.2). Then he quells all the turmoil of the passions and appetites expressed in stanza 20 in images of swift-winged birds, lions, stags and leaping roes and the ardors and fears of love. Deep essential peace is brought to the soul. Stanza 21 marks the beginning of the spiritual marriage.

We can only understand these verses as our experience grows, and this will be even more true as we consider the later stanzas of this poem.

> So little of this is describable that we would never succeed in fully explaining what takes place in the soul that has reached this happy state. If she attains the peace of God which, as the Church says, surpasses all understanding (Phil 4:7), all understanding will be inadequate and mute when it comes to explaining this peace. (Commentary on Stanza 21.15)

Nevertheless our spirit often goes before, taking hold of what the rest of us cannot yet grasp. Let us not think that we have attained to the spiritual marriage because we have a certain vision of what it may be. All the rest of our human organism has to be brought into conformity with what we have been shown. There is still work to do within the spiritual marriage.

Transformation and union

Cf.   *Canticle*, stanzas 23-40
      Commentary on these stanzas

"The bride has entered / The sweet garden of her desire." Stanza 22 marks the beginning of the spiritual marriage. This is "incomparably greater than the spiritual espousal, for it is a total transformation in the Beloved in which each surrenders the entire possession of self to the other with a certain consummation of the union of love" (Commentary on Stanza 22.3). Few of us, I imagine, can claim to have entered this place, yet that does not mean that there is nothing in these verses for us. It would be a pity to dismiss all that John says as something above and beyond us. If God is truly God and not a being made by us in our own image, there will always be areas of mystery which have not yet been opened to us. Nevertheless we can look toward them with a limited measure of understanding, for God does give us foretastes of union all along the way. Seen against our own lesser experiences, the characteristics of the spiritual marriage do not differ in kind but in quality of love. The principles of spiritual growth are the same for us all.

We see first of all that, in entering the garden, the soul meets the Bridegroom in the shadow of the tree of temptation which is also the tree of the cross.

Beneath the apple tree:
There I took You for my own,

There I offered You my hand,
And restored You,
Where your mother was corrupted.

(Stanza 23)

In time of temptation we may recognize fear and paranoia as the poisonous apples that are offered to us instead of the hand of the crucified Jesus. Choice is difficult when love is weak. Yet even within the spiritual marriage there is still the possibility of separation and the need for continual choice. For we are not completely transformed through our initial conversion but gradually perfected through successive experiences of the power of the cross. Through the cross Jesus offers his hand to the human race and every soul within it, through all the realities we experience in being incarnate beings. He offers his companionship through all those choices which may come to us a dozen times a day. If we choose with him, our potential for spiritual marriage is brought closer and intensified. We then come to feel that the language of *The Spiritual Canticle* is not as exaggerated as we may have thought.

In the succeeding verses John shows us the characteristics of unitive love. Stanza 25 speaks of its reliability and constancy. It is not volatile and effervescent like new wine or like the "touch of a spark." It is spiced, fermented wine "settled within the soul in spiritual substance and savor and good works." As John says, "These old lovers hardly ever fail God, for they now stand above all that would make them fail Him" (Commentary on Stanza 25.11).

It is the Holy Spirit who now pervades the soul with wisdom, penetrating to the innermost "wine-cellar" of her being. Here John gives another principle of spiritual growth. God's wisdom is not acquired through natural learning processes. "Naturally, it is impossible to love without first understanding what is loved, but supernaturally God can easily infuse and increase love without the infusion or increase of particular knowledge" (Commentary on Stanza 26.8). Through this infused wisdom the innocence of Eden is restored to the human soul. It is as if she can no longer understand evil nor judge anything in a bad light for "she does not have within herself the habit of evil by which to judge them" (Commentary on 26.14). This does not mean that the mature soul is naive. The little flame of her own intellectual knowledge and judgement is not quenched. But within the great light of God's wisdom she can judge with deeper insight and greater accuracy.

Stanza 27 underlines the fact that with practice, choosing alongside God becomes a habit. The effort and pain are no longer felt.

> As an imperfect soul is ordinarily inclined toward evil, at least in the first movements of its will, intellect, memory, and appetites, and as it has imperfections, so on the other hand the soul in this state ordinarily inclines and moves toward God in the first movements of its intellect, memory, will, and appetites because of the great help and stability it has in God and its perfect conversion toward good. (Commentary on Stanza 27.7)

We see the results of this in stanza 28. No longer is the soul's service of God mixed up with the need to satisfy her own creativity; she has no interests apart from his. All her latent powers and energies find their fulfillment in his service, whatever that may involve. So natural has this disposition of mind become that she "frequently works for God and is occupied in Him and in His affairs without ever thinking or being aware that she is doing so." "Now my every act is love. . . . All the ability of my soul and body move . . . in love and because of love" (Commentary on Stanza 28.5 and 8).

We have already thought how reconciling this love can be even though it may be expressed in hidden and seemingly unimportant ways. Yet in the spiritual order energy is radiated out into the whole Church through God's love working in individual Christian souls. Therefore, John says, "Great wrong would be done to a person who possesses some degree of this solitary love as well as to the Church, if we should urge him to become occupied in exterior or active things" (Commentary on Stanza 29.3).

Stanzas 32 and 33 remind us of what we have heard before, that is God's contemplation of us rather than our contemplation of him that will heal and transform us. If we believe this it will affect the whole orientation of our prayer. Instead of straining to find God, disappointed and complaining of darkness when we experience nothing, we open ourselves up to his gaze. It is not easy to remain still as one by one our deceits and dishonesties come to the surface to be healed. In fact, as William Blake points out, it is a lifetime's work. "And we are put on earth a little space / That we may learn to bear the beams of love." In the spiritual marriage we shall be able to walk freely and happily under the open sky, not hiding ourselves from the sight of God like Adam and Eve.

The last five stanzas of *The Spiritual Canticle* were written four years later than the rest, doubtless because John's own vision now extended beyond the spiritual marriage in this life to the life that lies ahead. In stanza 36 he tells us that we shall not only be like God but will share his hidden secrets. These are the great mountains of the knowledge of God himself and the lesser hills of his wisdom revealed in created beings, words and decrees. In this life we have to press on through "thickets" of difficult doctrines which try our faith. Then, there is the promise that we shall understand the "mystery of the harmony between God's justice and mercy with respect to the manifestations of His judgements in the salvation of the human race" (Commentary on Stanza 37.3).

Then our deepest and most troubling questions will be answered. "There You will show me / What my soul has been seeking" (stanza 38). That "what" is summed up in stanza 39. John says that it is the breath of the Holy Spirit from God to the soul and from the soul to God; it is rejoicing in the fruition of God; it is the knowledge of creatures and their orderly arrangement; it is the pure and clear contemplation of the divine essence and finally total transformation in the immense love of God (see Commentary on Stanza 39.2).

Let us not turn away from this vision as something too high and remote from us. Since every other human desire and instinct has its fulfillment, we may believe that the divine seed planted within us at our creation also has its blossoming and fruition.

In stanza 40 John lists the solid but unromantic qualities that the soul may now hope to find within herself. They include freedom from desire for things "above and below" which are not in God's plan for her; final victory over the devil; the quietening of the passions of joy, hope, fear and sorrow in the soul; and the proper enjoyment of spiritual things by the purified senses.

John ends with a prayer for all of us who have set out on this inner journey. "May the most sweet Jesus, Bridegroom of faithful souls, be pleased to bring all who invoke His name to this glorious marriage. To Him be honor and glory, together with the Father and the Holy Spirit, *in saecula saeculorum.* Amen" (Commentary on Stanza 40.7).

The Living Flame of Love

1. O living flame of love
   That tenderly wounds my soul
   In its deepest center! Since
   Now You are not oppressive,
   Now Consummate! If it be Your will:
   Tear through the veil of this sweet encounter!

2. O sweet cautery,
    O delightful wound!
    O gentle hand! O delicate touch
    That tastes of eternal life
    And pays every debt!
    In killing You changed death to life.

3. O lamps of fire!
    In whose splendors
    The deep caverns of feeling,
    Once obscure and blind,
    Now give forth, so rarely and exquisitely,
    Both warmth and light to their Beloved.

4. How gently and lovingly
    You wake in my heart,
    Where in secret You dwell alone;
    And in Your sweet breathing,
    Filled with good and glory,
    How tenderly You swell my heart with love!

Cf.   Prologue; stanza 1.1-6; 15-17; 21-23; stanza 2.1: 10-16;
       stanza 3.1-5; 14-17

It is easier for a writer on spiritual themes to describe the journey rather than the arrival. For we are all children of process and can only know through faith that there is a fulfillment of our desires and a reply to our questionings. The confidence with which John writes of the spiritual marriage and the life of transformation is for him too the result of faith rather than direct vision. Yet the foretastes of eternal life that he has known have been a pledge of the truth of all Christ's promises in the gospels. *The Living Flame of Love* is in one aspect a prolonged meditation on John 14:23: "If a man loves me he will keep my word and my Father will love him and we will come to him and make our abode with him." It is not academic and unreal that the Trinity of persons desires to find a home in our human hearts. John is telling us, insofar as another human being can, what a difference that indwelling will make in our daily lives.

His treatise was written for a friend and disciple, Dona Ana de Penalosa. Not everyone, he realized, would have understood him, and he tells those who "do not relish this language God speaks within them" not to be dismissive of the experience of those who do (Commentary on Stanza 1.6). Few of us can claim to know and love as John did, but if we want it our capacity will grow. For "with time and practice, love can receive added quality . . . and become more intensified" (Prologue, 3).

In this poem the whole Trinity is at work within the human soul. In the second book of *The Dark Night* we were shown the burning log as an image of purification; now it is used to describe transformation and union. In stanza 1 the living flame is identified with those sudden awakenings and flashes of the Spirit which may come to us at any time if God is in the ground of our hearts and wills.

> Hence we can compare the soul in its ordinary condition in this state of transformation of love to the log of wood that is ever immersed in fire, and the acts of this soul to the flame that blazes up from the fire of love. The more intense the fire of union, the more vehemently does this fire burst into flames. (Commentary on Stanza 1.4)

These acts are gifts which we cannot produce through our own efforts. C. S. Lewis was "surprised by joy" when they came to him unexpectedly. Occasionally some apparently dry doctrine about God, the world or the Church will reveal itself in its living aspect. The times and places in which they occur become indelibly imprinted on our memory, for they are a part of the incarnation of the vision. It is impossible to convey to others what we have felt so surely. There is a certain hop garden in which I suddenly became vividly aware of God as the source of my life. He/she was neither male nor female but Someone in a place where these concepts meet. The realization came in a breath of freshness; the universe seemed to expand and the surrounding natural world to watch and participate. I felt an enhanced sense of my own worth and that of every living thing around. It is true that this particular "awakening" need not necessarily have been a Christian one; yet because I am a Christian it was so. John says that such acts are communicated to the soul in its deepest place where the devil cannot enter. Therefore they are divine.

> And it should not be held as incredible in a soul now examined, purged and tried in the fire of tribulations, trials and many kinds of temptations, and found faithful in love, that the promise of the Son of God be fulfilled, the promise that the Most Blessed Trinity will come and dwell within anyone who loves Him. (Commentary on Stanza 1.15)

In the end, he says, only the thin veil of dying will separate us from God.

Such experiences are very different from those sought for and discovered through drugs and psychological techniques. It is true that these have power to tear open the consciousness and reveal hitherto unknown spiritual and psychic powers within the unconscious. But if the tearing open is self-induced or forced it may come too soon and too violently, revealing an inner darkness and chaos which techniques may suppress but have no power to heal. Only the love of God can safely and surely awaken the spiritual capacities that we certainly have within us. Then we come to know ourselves, not as "perfect" people in isolation, but with others within the ocean of trinitarian love. "It seems to it [the soul] that the entire universe is a sea of love in which it is engulfed, for, conscious of the living point or center of love within itself, it is unable to catch sight of the boundaries of this love" (Commentary on Stanza 2.10). We do not blind ourselves to the troubles and injustices of the world or even the suffering resulting from natural disasters which may seem to be directly inflicted by God. The ultimate stumbling block to faith is not the trouble that can be traced to human sin, but rather the avalanche which can suddenly destroy a village or the rain that does not fall. Yet faith looks through the darkness to a God who also suffers to bring healing and transformation where none could have been expected.

Stanza 3 tells us that each one of us has something unique and special to give back to God. We have "lamps of fire" within us, lamps of goodness, justice, fortitude, mercy and wisdom. The light and warmth of these qualities come from God, but in us they can be given back enhanced as a gift to him. "The soul reflects the divine light in a more excellent way because of the active intervention of its will" (Commentary on Stanza 3.77). What you and I do as persons does make a difference in the scheme of things. So John says that "a reciprocal love is thus actually formed between God and the soul like the marriage union and surrender, in which the goods of both . . . are possessed by both together" (Commentary on Stanza 3.79).

Stanza 4 tells of the deep communion of the soul with the indwelling Word of God and of the solitude and silence which are the necessary setting for our awakenings. This does not necessarily now involve physical solitude but freedom of heart. "It is in that soul in which less of its own appetites and pleasures dwell that He dwells more alone, more pleased and more as though in His own house ruling and governing it" (Commentary on Stanza 4.14).

Out of this place of habitual union the flames of actual union arise. Out of them is born a new insight into created things.

In this awakening they not only seem to move, but they likewise disclose the beauties of their being, power, loveliness and graces, and the root of their duration and life. For the soul is conscious of how all creatures, earthly and heavenly, have their life, duration and strength in Him. . . . And here lies the remarkable delight of this awakening. *The soul knows creatures through God and not God through creatures.* (Commentary on Stanza 4.5)

This insight makes all the difference to our active ministry, whatever form it may take. Only in God can we begin to see other beings as they really are. Only in God can we give them the reverence which they deserve.

The end of John's poem celebrates the freedom of life in the Holy Spirit, that freedom and joy which we taste consciously in our moments of awakening. Let us remember on the many days when life seems hard and monotonous that the same life is still present unseen and unknown within us. Although much of our life may be spent in the shadows, the sun continues to shine and is the source and reality of our being.

Epilogue

Universal Priesthood

Cf. *Night* II.xi.4
"Mine are the heavens and mine is the earth"
("Prayer of a Soul Taken with Love" in *Sayings of Life and Love*)
Stanza 28 of *The Spiritual Canticle*
together with John's Commentary on Stanza 29.1-3

In the scattered references given here we find teaching which is otherwise often more implicit than explicit in John's writings. He shows us that concentration on individual perfection is not the end, for trinitarian life is of its nature communal. As we grow into this life we discover in ourselves an increasing longing for the reconciliation of all things in Christ. Our right concern for ourselves becomes part of a whole in which there is no separation or conflict of interest.

On this earth we begin to learn our vocation as priests of creation, no matter what our particular vocation in the Church and world may be. The ordained ministry represents but does not supersede this universal priesthood. In Christ all Christians share in the sacerdotal and pastoral work which he showed forth in his high-priestly prayer before his passion: "For their sake I consecrate myself that they also may be consecrated in truth" (Jn 17:19); "Holy Father, keep them in your name which you have given me that they may be one" (Jn 17:11). It is the ever-renewed consecration of our whole being on the altar of our lives that makes our pastoral ministry fruitful.

As we look at the first reference from John of the Cross we find that contrary to what we may have thought, this gift of self does not necessarily demand a stripping away of human gifts and potentialities until we reach a naked center capable of being united to a naked God. We read instead of a gathering up by God of the soul with all its talents "that the energy and power of the whole harmonious composite may be employed in this love." Despite the dismissive references to love of created beings which we find elsewhere in John's works, that love is now placed where it belongs. The soul finds its fulfillment in the first great commandment *"which neither disdaining anything human nor excluding it from this love* states: You shall love your God with your whole heart and with your whole mind and with your whole soul and with all your strength'" (*Night,* II.xi.4).

It is this offering and the continual purification that it involves which can be used by God as he gives the world back to us for our service and enjoyment. "Mine are the nations, the just are mine and mine the sinners. The angels are mine, and the Mother of God, and all things are mine; and God Himself is mine and for me, because Christ is mine and all for me" (*Sayings of Light and Love*). It is only when we get our priorities wrong that our work for others becomes social service rather than part of our Christian prayer.

It is true nevertheless that at different times and occasions pastoral rather than sacerdotal elements may be most prominent in our lives. In the Commentary on Stanza 29 of *The Spiritual Canticle* John gives advice to those who are actively employed in pastoral service.

Let those, then, who are singularly active, who think they can win the world with their preaching and exterior works, observe that here they would profit the

Church and please God much more . . . were they to spend at least half of this time with God in prayer. . . . They would then certainly accomplish more, and with less labor, by one work than they otherwise would by a thousand. . . . Without prayer they would do a great deal of hammering but accomplish little, and sometimes nothing, and even at times cause harm.

God forbid that the salt should begin to lose its savor (Mt 5:13), for however much they may appear to achieve externally, they will in substance be accomplishing nothing; it is beyond doubt that good works can be performed only by the power of God. (Commentary on *Canticle*, stanza 29.3)

However, John is more concerned with those who for one reason or another are drawn toward the priestly offering of hidden love, a vocation which in the West is often vulnerable and open to attack. Yet there comes a time in every life when we have nothing left to give if we have not this. Outward achievement may no longer be possible when we are removed from the mainstream of life through accident, sickness, increasing age or other cause. Then, when we have no particular ministry, everything and everyone becomes our concern. Our offering in Christ's offering and within his Body can flow toward those whom we shall never see and who will never know us in the flesh. It is part of the dark night of faith that we may rarely see visible results and yet believe that what we are and do makes a difference in the scheme of things.

> Now I occupy my soul
> And all my energy in His service
> I no longer tend the herd
> Nor have any other work
> Now that my every act is love.
>
> (*Canticle*, stanza 28)

It is true that for most of us, most of the time, there is a herd to tend, and it is right that it should be so. And if we find the early stages of John's scheme of spiritual training too cut-and-dried, too much like a grammar of the soul, this may be necessary if our outward acts are to be those of love. With that discipline we can hope to be less concerned about where we are on the ladder of success and more capable of keeping our priorities right.

In our work for reconciliation, prayer is the one human activity which can embrace everyone all the time. In everything else we have to leave one person or work or culture in order to give ourselves to another. It is true that as we immerse ourselves in each concern it can become a sacrament of the whole, but it can never itself be that whole. Our embrace of the wholeness can only be found through God's embrace of us.

So we come to the end of John's account of the mysterious inner journey of the soul in response to God's calling. We may now ask ourselves how this is going to affect our everyday lives. Of course, it will have no effect unless it is used as a way of life. But if we try to follow John's counsel we may hope to see changes taking place in our inner world.

In trying to let go of our possessiveness of people and things and allow them to be more fully themselves, we shall find a freedom in relationships that are no longer dominated by personal needs and desires.

As we learn to see our lives as one whole in which both darkness and light have their part, we shall begin to accept that suffering is not intended as a punishment but as an education. Most of us need a trusted friend at this point to help us dig out those hidden pockets of repression which conserve fear and anger and fragment our inner lives.

The very difficulty of this process will help us to grow in compassion and humanity. We may hope to become more capable of sharing in Christ's work of dying and rising to bring new life into the world. In this we shall find our union with God. "If a man loves me he will keep my word, and my Father will love him, and we will come to him and make our home with him" (Jn 14:23).

Basically, circumstances do not matter. Whoever or wherever we may be, we have the opportunity to become true children of God and co-workers with him. John of the Cross sees this as the destiny of every Christian soul and in his teaching guides us along the paths of ordinary human experience toward our common goal.

Acknowledgements

I wish to express my gratitude to the Institute of Carmelite Studies in Washington, D.C., for permission to use material from the Kavanaugh/Rodriguez translation of *The Works of John of the Cross.*

Thanks are also due to the Rev. Dr. E. W. Trueman Dicken for permission to use his translation of the original sketch of Mount Carmel by John of the Cross, which first appeared in his book *The Crucible of Love* (London: Darton, Longman and Todd, 1963).

Thanks too to Sister Jane SLG and Sister Cintra OSH, who read the first draft of this book and made helpful suggestions; to Alma Corry, who typed the manuscript, and to Sister Christine SLG for much practical help and encouragement.

The Prayers of John of the Cross

Alphonse Ruiz, O.C.D. (ed.)

ISBN 1-56548-073-2
paper, 5 3/8 x 8 1/2, 128 pp., **3d printing**

The Prayers of Teresa of Avila

Thomas Alvarez, O.C.D. (ed.)

ISBN 1-56548-065-1
paper, 5 3/8 x 8 1/2, 136 pp., **4th printing**

Therese of Lisieux—A Discovery of Love
Selected Spiritual Writings

Terence Carey, O.C.D. (ed.)

ISBN 1-56548-072-4
paper, 5 3/8 x 8 1/2, 144 pp., **3d printing**

In Search of God
Meditation in the Christian Tradition

by W. Herbstrith (with Teresa of Avila, John of the Cross,
Therese of Lisieux, Edith Stein)

ISBN 1-56548-067-8
paper, 5 1/8 x 8, 128 pp., **4th printing**

From Ash to Fire—A Contemporary Journey
through the Interior Castle of Teresa of Avila

by Carolyn Humphreys

ISBN 1-56548-040-6
paper, 5 3/8 x 8 1/2, 160 pp., **3d printing**